"The pervasive damaging effects of father ab[...] distance on children have been well substantiated. While the facts are known, the human truths are in the details. Through graphic case histories and her own personal story, Dr. Beth Erickson documents the impact of father loss on both males and females. No other book offers a more thorough treatment of this subject."

James L. Framo, Ph.D., A.B.P.P.
Author, *Family-of-Origin Therapy*

"It is a cruel lie that children don't need fathers. In recent decades, this irresponsible notion has devastated many lives, if not society as a whole. Dr. Beth Erickson uses her uncommon sense and sensibility to illuminate the many faces of father hunger. Her practical and heartfelt recommendations will surely relieve some of the crippling pain of this societal tragedy."

Frank S. Pittman III, M.D.
Author, *Man Enough: Fathers, Sons and the Search for Masculinity* and *Grow Up!*

"*Longing for Dad* perceptively focuses on father loss, its impact and its remedy. We all desire our children to become happy, positive and healthy adults. Our children will be the beneficiaries of the ideas in this book."

Patricio M. Serna
Justice, New Mexico Supreme Court
Former Chief Family Court Judge, First Judicial District of New Mexico

"As a psychologist, I often approach issues from a purely psychological perspective. This book allowed me to connect with the spiritual parts of myself that are often out of my awareness. . . . I came out stronger, more connected with the 'lost father' in myself."

Denise Twohey, Ed.D.
Professor of Counseling Psychology, University of North Dakota

"Dr. Erickson has vividly integrated her personal experience and professional expertise to create a powerful examination of the effects of father loss and how this terrible loss can be healed. Her approach is wholistic and systemic, and thankfully, she is bold enough to address the all-important spiritual dimensions of the subject."

Paul E. Hopkins, D.Min.
Executive Director, Samaritan Counseling Center, Albuquerque, NM

LONGING FOR

DAD

FATHER LOSS AND
ITS IMPACT

Beth M. Erickson, Ph.D.

Health Communications, Inc.
Deerfield Beach, Florida

www.hci-online.com

Library of Congress Cataloging-in-Publication Data

Erickson, Beth M.
    Longing for dad : father loss and its impact / Beth M. Erickson.
        p.   cm.
    Includes bibliographical references and index.
    ISBN 1-55874-549-1 (pbk.)
        1. Paternal deprivation.   2. Fatherless family.   3. Loss
    (Psychology) in children.   4. Loss (Psychology)—Problems, exercises,
    etc.   I. Title.
BF723.P33E55   1998   98-15536
155.9'3—dc21   CIP

©1998 Beth M. Erickson

ISBN 1-55874-549-1

Publisher: Health Communications, Inc.
                3201 S.W. 15th Street
                Deerfield Beach, FL 33442-8190

Cover design by Lawna Patterson Oldfield
Cover photos ©PhotoDisc 1998

***In Memoriam**

*To Rudolph Julius Erickson (1904–1954)
and Mildred Rask Erickson (1906–1982),
from whom I got so many supplies
for growing up a caring and competent
human being.*

Contents

Part Three: Remedies and Recovery

Preface

This is a book about the importance of fathers in children's lives.

When I finished my first book—which was also about men—in 1993, I knew it would not be the last one I would write. Nor, I hope, will this one. In order to seek direction and input on my second book, I invited a handful of former clients to join me in a focus group over coffee and muffins on a Saturday morning. Who would be more familiar with my work and the ideas I was passionate about? All of them avid readers, they also provided an invaluable finger on the pulse of interesting subjects. When I asked them what topics they thought needed to be addressed, they each told me that their relationship—or lack of one—with their father had affected them profoundly, for better or for worse. They suggested that I write a book about this—the idea for *Longing for Dad* was born.

Their idea struck a chord within me: Because my relationship with my father and his untimely death had such an impact on me, I knew that I could maintain my interest in and commitment to the project. As I began researching the topic,

I realized that the incidence and effects of father loss went far beyond what I had initially imagined. I concluded that we in this country are rearing the neediest generation that America has ever seen, with father loss being a major contributor to this condition. I also could see that, in my role as family psychologist, I was in a unique position to do both primary prevention to educate people about their choices, as well as to intervene to help people heal. Hence, the thrust of this book.

Acknowledgments

No major project can be completed in a vacuum, and this book is no exception. I am grateful to many people for their contribution to the conception and birth of this book. First and foremost, I must thank my psychotherapy clients and university students. I am particularly indebted to that original focus group of former patients who nudged me to eventually give birth to these ideas. My clients' courage to struggle and the wisdom we all developed as a result have been constant sources of inspiration and encouragement to me. Their questions and their words—many of which are sprinkled throughout this book—have led me to find answers to very painful and ponderous questions. For the support and contributions of all these wonderful people I am sincerely grateful.

The person who deserves the next largest amount of credit is David Walther, my life partner, unofficial editor, cheerleader, and the wind beneath my wings. He has always understood the personal meaning of this project. As a family lawyer, he also has grasped the potential of this book to prevent and to remediate the damage he sees in his office daily. He has read every draft enthusiastically, tirelessly and, often, more than once. I often wonder whether this book would have been possible without him.

Various friends and colleagues also have been a great help. From reading drafts to helping me hone and advocate my ideas, their contributions have been invaluable. Everyone should be so lucky as to count these people as friends and colleagues! Those generous and supportive folks are: Cathy Swedelius, Karen Lewis, David Handley, Shirley Scott, Jim Loughren, Denise Twohey, Richard Fields, Cheryl Karp, Egon Dumler, Marge Prefontaine, Frank Pittman, Charme Davidson, Bill Ress, Paul Wirtz, Judi Sczymanski, Glenn Swedelius, Faye Seeman and John Walther.

The people at Health Communications have been wonderful to work with. I would commend them to any author. First and foremost is Gary Seidler, the publisher who sold me on HCI. A true visionary, his personal mark on this book is that he "got it" from the beginning. He truly has been chicken soup for my author's soul. And his staff has also been bright and accommodating, especially Christine Belleris, Lorrie Keip and Suzanne Smith. Jan Werblin's editorial contribution to the finished product has been invaluable.

Finally, my two golden retrievers and two cats have been a constant source of companionship and peacefulness in the often solitary process of writing this book. The dogs have lain under my desk and the cats on it while I clicked out each syllable. They are great friends who offer unconditional comfort and love, and I love them dearly.

Introduction

*Hope is the feeling you have that
the feeling you have
isn't permanent.*

—Jean Kerr
Finishing Touches

This book is for adults who as children experienced "father loss," a condition wherein their father was literally absent from their life or was physically present but was emotionally unavailable to them. Children who have grown up without an actual or emotional relationship with their birth father are traumatized by their father's absence. While the loss of a father to death is an obvious trauma to children, they may also experience father loss from not knowing their father, from having an inadequate father or from having lost day-to-day contact with him. Paradoxically, the trauma caused to children by father loss is usually more severe than having no father at all, and the impact of his absence is more damaging than if he were present but unloving.

Both men and women unknowingly haul this emotional baggage from their early childhood experience into adulthood.

Throughout their lives the effects of father loss often show up in such seemingly unrelated issues as: fear of commitment, professional or academic failure, various addictions, and general malaise and melancholy.

The concept that fathers are as important as mothers in children's lives may seem politically incorrect. Children's connections with their father is perhaps the most underrated, least understood relationship in life. It has been assumed within the last few decades in psychology, and increasingly in the culture at large, that mothers are more important to children than fathers. This belief creates twin misconceptions. One is that mothers are to blame whenever anything goes wrong in the lives of their children, with the concept of the "schizophrenogenic mother" being the quintessential example. The other fallacy is that fathers are irrelevant, disposable and superfluous. Neither of these beliefs serves children or families. And neither is accurate.

Although some people deny that fathers are significant to children and may even believe that fathers are a luxury, I know differently, from both a personal and a professional viewpoint. I know from my own experience that the traumatic loss of my father, when I was too young to do well without him, has affected every facet of my life. As a therapist, I've helped countless clients exhume and finally put to rest events in their lives that they have tried in vain to bury.[1] Throughout this, I have grown to understand the importance of a father to a child's life.

---

1. Each client granted permission to use their story in this book. While the stories are based on actual experiences, names and identifying information have been changed to protect their privacy.

This book has several purposes. One is to help readers recognize whether they suffer from father loss. If their loss happened long ago, it has likely slipped into the dark corners of their mind, where most would prefer it to stay. While they know something is wrong, they are at a loss to figure out what. For the male who has never felt man enough, no matter how hard he tries, this book provides answers to the question, *Why not?* It also offers suggestions for how he can remedy this painful condition. For the female who twists herself like a pretzel in relationships to avoid being alone, this book offers explanations for her self-defeating behavior and provides options for correcting it.

Parents and prospective parents will find this book helpful in their efforts to prevent harm to the next generation. While, of course, adults have the right to self-determination, it is important that they grasp, for their children and for the culture as a whole, the implications of their choices. This book is designed to help readers think about what they can do to help themselves with father loss, or how counseling or therapy might help them. The book also offers some nonblaming explanations for a father's apparent disinterest. Most children whose fathers are aloof or absent unfortunately conclude that they themselves are not good enough to warrant his staying, rather than knowing that his failing is just that: *his* failing. Instead, children who are abandoned or rejected by their father generally learn to feel flawed, unlovable, not good enough. This book will help readers begin to unwind the tangled reasoning they developed as children to explain the unexplainable: why their father didn't seem to love them enough to *stay* and love them.

Other readers will pick up this book because, for reasons of

finances, schedules, geographic isolation or their own internal
prohibitions, they simply are unable to avail themselves of outside, therapeutic help. And still other readers will be mental
health counselors and therapists who were not taught about the
identification and management of this very subtle and sensitive
clinical issue in graduate school, but who recognize the need to
help themselves and their own clients do this work. It is for
each of these kinds of audiences that this book is intended.

I have divided this book into three parts. Part 1 defines the
term "father loss," explains where it gets its power and what
causes it. In chapter 1, "My Story," I share with you my
experience with losing my father when I was young and how
that affected every facet of my life.

Chapter 2, "Father Loss and Father Hunger," defines "father
hunger" and ends with an exercise to help you understand the
role your father's presence or absence played in your life.
Chapter 3, "Father Absence and Child Development," summa-
rizes how a child's way of thinking often compounds the damage of father loss. Understanding children's reasoning is
necessary to grasp how their illogical logic and natural self-
centeredness predispose them to dysfunction in their life.
Chapter 4, "Seven Sources of Father Hunger," discusses the
sources of father hunger: death, divorce, single mothering,
adoption, addiction, abuse and traditional fathering.

Part 2 details the impact of father loss. Chapter 5, "When
Dick and Jane Grow Up," examines how each sex reacts to a
father's abandonment. Each sex is susceptible to certain types
of damage depending upon the socialized messages they
receive from the culture around them. Chapter 6, "Come Here,
Go Away," reveals the problems that people will likely have in
their marriages or significant relationships if they experienced

father loss. Chapter 7, "Spiritual Issues and Father Loss," highlights the philosophical and spiritual issues accompanying father loss that are magnified when an earthly parent is untrustworthy.

Part 3 offers solutions to begin healing. Chapter 8, "Taking the Bite Out of Father Hunger," offers self-help strategies to those who suffer from father loss. Chapter 9, "Both Fathers and Mothers Are Important," focuses on the critical role that each parent plays in a child's life.

Because I hope that therapists will also find this book useful, I have included a section especially for them. The appendixes contain some of my favorite, tried-and-true treatment strategies for therapists.

I hope to inspire personal reflection in all who read this book. To set the stage for your self-exploration, I've included action exercises intended to spark your thinking and to help you find personal meaning in the book. I urge you to keep a journal beside you as you read. Pause from time to time to take notes on those sections that hit you, on your thoughts as you read, and on your responses to the exercises and questions. Next to seeing a good therapist, I know of no better strategy for helping yourself than journaling.

PART ONE

Father Loss

1 My Story: Caught in a Conspiracy of Silence

*Families engage in a conspiracy
of silence around death. . . . In their efforts
to contain grief, the pain is actually
intensified as people wall off parts
of themselves. This avoidance of open,
shared grieving has its roots in the
losses of previous generations.*

—Murray Bowen, M.D.
Family Therapy in Clinical Practice

I was born the youngest of eight children in a traditional Scandinavian family. My mother was a second-generation Norwegian immigrant, and my father was a first-generation Swedish immigrant whose oldest brother was born in the old country. Of all the adjectives that could be used to describe both of these similar but

3

distinct ethnic groups, "stoic" is perhaps most apt. In addition, both of my parents' families were farmers for generations, whose way of life was characterized by rugged individualism and independence. Yet, despite the silent injunctions accompanying these traits that shaped our behavior and governed the way we managed our emotions, my family was a curious and paradoxical mixture of reserve and warmth, independence and closeness. We were expected to keep our problems to ourselves, but we could and did draw great strength from just being with each other. That is, as long as we made no attempt to talk about our feelings and problems.

My father was a Main Street businessman in our tiny Midwestern town. He owned and operated a creamery, as did four of his six brothers. Because he, too, was the youngest of eight, he worked hard to compete with his siblings and usually won the butter-making contests that he and his four brothers entered. To keep up with (or to best) his brothers, he usually worked six days a week. This also allowed him to fulfill the traditional role of father as provider. He thus was able to keep the wolves from the door and to feed the ten mouths that were dependent on him. We grew up poor, but I was oblivious to this at the time because the warmth, caring and closeness in our home compensated for the lack of money. My older sister would refer to our family's bond by saying again and again, "I'm glad we had babies instead of bicycles." From this, I learned that the investment of time in one's family truly can give the richest return, and even today, I am a "homebody," preferring to be home with my partner and our animals to being anywhere else.

Despite the long hours Daddy worked, he was a good dad to me. I always experienced a special closeness with him. This bond apparently went back before I have conscious memory. Mother lovingly and repeatedly told the story that I sang before I talked, shocking the family when, without having previously uttered a word, I sang all the words to a song, on pitch, from beginning to end. It was a lullaby about Daddy. By elementary school, Daddy and I were buddies. When the family visited friends past my bedtime, Daddy would lovingly put his sleepy little blond girl to bed, while the older kids were on their own. Those of you who grew up in a small town probably remember the town's whistle. Because it blew at noon, 6:00 and 9:30 P.M., it provided a structure that appealed to the highly organized Scandinavian and German immigrants

The author, age five, with her father, R. J. Erickson, age forty-six, at their home in Trimont, Minnesota, in 1950, four years before he passed away.

who populated most of our town. Wherever children were playing, we knew the rule: "Come home when the whistle blows." On my way, I would stop by Daddy's creamery, wait for him to lock up and walk the two blocks home with him. This routine almost became ritual. I remember nothing substantive in our conversations, but there didn't have to be. This was our alone time. I relished it and basked in it. To this day, I can hear the sounds of the stones crunching under the weight of his sturdy Swedish frame as we walked. Daddy clearly enjoyed our time together, as well.

Three months after my ninth birthday, my father was hospitalized for a serious, though not life-threatening, illness. Because the decision to hospitalize him was made suddenly as his chronic condition worsened, I was unable to say goodbye to him. Clearly, no one had any indication that he would not return; he merely had to leave for a while. In fact, I have no conscious memory of the last time I saw him. My first memory of his absence was being called out of school with my three older sisters and told by the town busybody that my daddy was dead.

Heart attack—ten minutes from the first pains until he was pronounced dead—at age fifty.

A family's style in dealing with emotions in general will have a great deal to do with how they deal with any loss, particularly the loss of someone as important as a father. As was apparent in my family, this style develops out of a family's unspoken expectations or rules and governs how children will deal with the emotional or actual absence of their father. In my own case, I knew I was to be impassive.

I remember crying only once after Daddy died. I had no doubt that I was to be a stoic little trouper, and that's what I was. Baffled and frightened by corpses and death, I remember sitting next to Mother but laying my head on my sister's lap in the front row at his funeral. I was afraid to peek up and see his dead body lying cold in the casket in his navy blue Sunday suit. So my last memory of my beloved daddy was seeing his nose as it protruded over the edge of the coffin as the head of this now strange, waxen figure lay cradled on its satin pillow. And I remember standing numb and dumbstruck at the cemetery, as icy November Minnesota winds swirled leaves around us. Already I was beginning to seal over parts of my psyche and my soul.

And that was that.

I went back to school the afternoon of his funeral because, after all, I had missed a lot of school and I had a lot of catching up to do. I sat at the dining room table that night, doing homework, and apparently no one thought it unusual. No one recognized the danger in my coping so "well," because we had already made a silent pact to keep our feelings to ourselves. So I, the stoic little trooper that I was expected to be, trekked on as the family silently decreed.

I remember only one attempt to explain to me what death was and where Daddy had gone. Unfortunately, that was during an argument between my two teenage sisters about whether Daddy was in heaven with Jesus and the angels or not. (My sisters were fundamentalist and Unitarian even before they knew the difference!) I remember watching, puzzled, frozen, wanting them to shush so we wouldn't disturb Mother in the next room. Why were they arguing about this? All I wanted to know was where my daddy was, and no one would tell me!

It was not that I was ever told directly not to discuss Daddy or my feelings about him. And it was not that we had no feelings or that we did not love each other. I realize now that our conspiracy of silence was in part because of our ethnic background and partly to protect Mother. In retrospect, I am certain that we believed that if we grieved openly, then the matriarch of our clan would be sad. Somehow I knew that making Mother sad was to be avoided at all costs.

It is impossible for children not to have a reaction to grief, despite how "well" they appear to be coping. In fact, if children manage too well prematurely, most can expect later problems. When left alone to grapple with a father's emotional or literal absence, children have various feelings. They may feel responsible and give up their own childhood to become a little adult. They may feel a sense of urgency to protect their remaining parent so they don't lose her, too, and yet be ashamed of these needy juvenile feelings. They may feel helpless and guilty because they feel required to do something, but they don't know what or how. Or they may develop their own problems to distract themselves and everyone else from the grief. Or they may simply withdraw from the pain or rebel at the weight of it. Each of these responses signals that the child is in trouble.

I coped by submerging my own needs and feelings. For a few months after the funeral, Mother had me sleep in her bed at night. And every night it was the same. Mama's muffled sobs would wake me from a sound sleep, and I would lie frozen beside her. I hoped earnestly that she would not notice that I was awake, because I felt that I should say or do something, and I had no clue what would help. However, that didn't stop me from feeling responsible. Night after night, I would lie there in terror: that my stoic and reticent mother was so devastated; that I was completely lost about what I could or should do to help; and that somehow in her uncharacteristic show of emotion, I could lose the mother I knew, too. Then, the next morning, almost as if an iron curtain had dropped down, Mother would carry on as if neither her agony nor her expression of these emotions had happened. And I took my cues from her. We were to be impassive—and so we were. We were to take care of Mother so she could continue taking care of us—and so we did, each in our own way.

Although some people may wish to avoid the feelings involved in the emotional or literal absence of their father, it is not possible to do so permanently without paying a price. As Biff Loman, Arthur Miller's character in the play *Death of a Salesman,* said after experiencing both literal and emotional abandonment by his father, "Attention must be paid!" Try as they might, people cannot avoid dealing with father loss. If they attempt to avoid giving proper significance to this important relationship in their lives, they can expect to suffer the consequences in their psychological, relational, professional or spiritual lives. And if the consequences of their poor choices in these arenas don't catch up with them, then subsequent losses will.

For twenty-four years, I continued to meet my family's expectations in ways that would have made my dad proud. I kept my focus on intellectual pursuits and achievements. In high school, I was intent on being a good student and a leader. My major at the private college I attended required that I read two hundred pages per night just to keep up, and so I unquestioningly did. My first career was high school English teacher of both gifted and disturbed kids. After two of my students committed suicide, I began graduate school with the ostensible purpose of finding out how to help troubled students deal more effectively with their lives. With the benefit of twenty/twenty hindsight, I now see that this was the beginning of my own quest to piece together facets of myself I had blocked off years before in the service of my family, as these two students apparently felt they must. Only they made the ultimate sacrifice.

It was fortunate that I had already begun to be more introspective, because suddenly twenty-four years later, all that I had denied when Daddy died came crashing in on me. This was when my oldest sister, whose lap I had occupied during Daddy's funeral, suddenly died of an undiagnosed brain tumor that had grown like fingers all over her brain.

Dead at the age of forty-nine—two and a half days after her cancer was diagnosed at the Mayo Clinic.

Despite our sixteen-year age difference, Dorothy and I were close, like a favorite aunt and niece. When she died, I could not eat or sleep for a month and scarcely could work, despite my best efforts to be the trooper once again. I felt like a cannon had torn out my insides, leaving me an automaton to bounce off people and walls with no sense of direction. The constant pit in my stomach left me nauseated and would not subside. Although Dorothy and I clearly were close, my reaction seemed, even to me, to be extreme and out of proportion. Gradually, it began to dawn on me that the strength and depth of my response were related to that earlier, much more traumatic event: Daddy's death. Now, at the same time that I needed to grieve for my sister, the walls I had erected to protect myself from pain came crashing down as my sister's death set off reverberations of the unresolved loss of my father. I have since realized that current losses often reactivate prior unresolved losses, but at the time, I did not know what was happening to me. So, spontaneously and without warning, I began reliving Dad's death while I was still raw from my sister's. However, in order to allow myself to mourn for either of them, I first had to peel away years and layers of defenses that I had used to wallpaper over that first cataclysmic event. Those defenses had helped me to keep the crush of feelings that naturally accompanied my father's death out of sight and out of mind. I finally understood why I had hated fall. And I knew then that I needed to devise a ritual that finally would allow me to end my perpetual mourning.

Putting My Experiences to Work

My father's life and death have had a dramatic impact on me professionally. Obviously they are both the basis of and the reason for writing this book. As is true for most therapists, whether they know it (or like it) or not, my work has evolved out of my own experiences as a child and from how they have shaped my adult life. In my therapist's chair, my life with Daddy and my sudden and traumatic loss of him give me a third eye and ear for identifying and treating unresolved father issues. While other therapists who experienced no such trauma might miss the significance of a patient's life with or without a father, I have an internal Geiger counter that clicks noisily when I detect this issue embedded in the calamities that clients routinely bring to therapy. It often underlies their sexual dysfunction, low self-esteem, marital conflict, hopelessness and even their children's acting out. I also seldom have difficulty empathizing with clients who have made a mess of their lives; I have done some pretty stupid things to mess up my own life, primarily because of my imprint experiences in my family. Conversely, I know from firsthand experience that it is in identifying and resolving repressed, unfortunate childhood experiences that we find freedom. So approaching treatment from this camera angle allows me to help clients unfreeze their arrested psychological growth and development while they solve their current specific problem.

As a therapist, my approach centers around helping people recognize how the unspoken messages they got from their families shape their view of acceptable behavior. I applied this same approach to myself and began by drawing my genogram. A genogram is a chart of a family, including names, birth dates, death dates and causes of death. From this bare-bones information, a person can draw inferences that help highlight family patterns and explain their roots. I had gleaned enough information from Mother before she died to be able to draw our family for five generations. As I began drawing Mother's branch of the family, a very significant conclusion virtually jumped off the page. Finally, I could grasp why she handled us and Dad's death the way she did.

Mother had experienced four deaths in six and a half years by the time she was fifteen, and she was orphaned because of them. By the time I had experienced two sisters' deaths and faced my father's, I was in my middle thirties, was degreed in psychology and was a practicing psychotherapist. And I was reeling from the deaths, despite having acquired many tools for dealing with trauma. Mother didn't have those tools when her father died when she, too, was nine, followed within two years by the deaths of her mother and grandfather, who lived with them. The final blow was the accidental death of her beloved nineteen-year-old brother that triggered the sale of the family farm. At fifteen, Mother was both orphaned and homeless, and had to go out into the world to support herself. These events, combined with her already considerable Norwegian reserve, shut her down emotionally. Thus, it is no surprise that she would have great difficulty processing Dad's loss openly. Because my sister's death brought my dad's death to life for me, I finally understood that she must have sensed that openly grieving Dad's death could reactivate her previous losses. Her excruciating experiences in adolescence compelled her to keep this current loss out of sight and out of mind so that her other losses also could be kept at bay. Thus she developed the strong defense of denial against the personal holocaust in her adolescence that a fifteen-year-old is simply not equipped emotionally or intellectually to handle, especially not alone.

Finally realizing these factors resolved and erased any lingering anger I felt toward Mother for her handling of Dad's death. Thank heaven this happened before she died! It also allowed me to feel great empathy for her and to quit judging her as an inadequate parent. Little wonder she was unable to have a warm, empathic discussion with her children about death! It would have caused all of her own unhealed wounds to ache. Most important, it helped me stop trying to make her change so she would meet my needs better. This, of course, had the paradoxical effect of motivating her to try to meet my needs better, especially as she began to realize that these were some of the last gifts she could give me. This in turn further confirmed my resolve to approach my clients this way. When people stop blaming their parents for their shortcomings and instead can begin to understand and get themselves understood, they can begin to free themselves of the grip of traumatic experiences.

Lessons My Father Taught Me

I not only learned from tracing my mother's history. I also became aware of the many ways in which my father shaped my life, both deliberately and unintentionally. When I was six years old, I asked my father for a bicycle to replace the rusty hand-me-down my sisters rode. Before he agreed, he insisted that I earn and save my own money to help him buy it. Of the $40.00 it took to purchase my shiny blue Schwinn at the local hardware store, I contributed $3.46. And was I proud! As he taught me how to wrap packages of freshly made butter by hand, he simultaneously showed me the joys of cooperating with and working alongside another, the pleasures of contributing and how to cherish the moment no matter how ordinary. Daddy and Mama showed me faith by having my next older sister and me kneel before them to say nightly bedtime prayers, by praying before each meal and by letting our family Bible gather no dust.

But, as is true for most of us, not all the lessons I learned from my Dad were deliberately taught. And some were not positive. Yet, my father's life and death have molded every aspect of my life, for better and for worse.

The advantages I gained from his life and my relationship with him are many and significant. He kindled my motivation to achieve. I completed my Ph.D. from a prestigious university in record time. I conducted a dissertation study that advanced the knowledge in the field and then completed two years of postdoctoral training in family therapy at another fine university. He indirectly influenced my ultimate career direction. I not only became a psychologist; I specialize in families, gender and loss. And my father shaped *how* I work: long, hard and sometimes too much for my own good. The positive side of this ethic taught me to be industrious and to never say "can't." The phrase "Anything worth doing is worth doing right" was virtually a family mantra.

My relationship with my father has also molded my view of myself as a woman. His appreciation of me as a little girl gave me a belief that I can be appreciated as an adult female.

My relationship with Daddy and the love and admiration my mother had for him even after he had died affect what I want and expect out of my significant relationships. My preference for intimate, eye-to-eye contact, my ability to experience pleasure and connection from everyday experiences, and my love of giving and receiving affection come directly from my interactions with Dad. And my love of admiring the man I love comes directly from my relationship with my father. As a little girl, I used to love to watch him shave and then splash on Old Spice when he finished. I also learned to admire my man from what I observed between my parents. Mother talked virtually until the day she died about how she loved Daddy at first sight when they met when she was nineteen.

Both of my parents strongly believed in and taught the Golden Rule and personal integrity. From them, I learned that my word is my bond. They were guileless almost to the point of naiveté, which I can be, too. My parents were leaders in their community and generous stewards of their time, talents and money, despite their limited funds. Daddy's and my last act before coming home from the creamery on Saturday evenings was to deliver to our church's pastor a fresh chicken, a dozen eggs and a pound of butter.

In sum, I learned: to try to leave the world a better place for my having been in it; to enjoy the simple things, like Sunday afternoon family drives into the country followed by ice cream cones all around; to love unabashedly and openly; to recognize the importance of hard work and persistence for getting the good things in life; and to appreciate the multiple pleasures in closeness and in meeting challenges.

However, I also developed less desirable traits from my relationship with my dad, from his death and from my family's interaction patterns. Daddy's sudden and untimely death caused me to choose men who ultimately will abandon me, emotionally or literally. Unfortunately, being abandoned feels familiar and "right," and probably more than anything accounts for my divorces. And yet, I am terrified of being abandoned, a fear that I struggle to manage so it doesn't manage me. This fear of being left (which came both from Daddy and, in effect, my whole family) made it difficult for me to learn to stand on my own finally and to face my fears of loneliness and separations. This terror was also part of my poor choices in relationships with men. Further, my taking care of Daddy taught me to continue this in relationships with men, and my paralysis at taking care of Mother after Dad's death also prompts me to be a caretaker of women. However, I finally have learned to abide by the rule I devised to protect myself from this tendency: No longer will I take sole responsibility for the maintenance of relationships. Because of my family's expectation that we deny our emotions, denial became a way of life. So reality testing was a skill and an attitude that I had to learn slowly and painstakingly.

In short, as with most people, I had a mix of good and bad experiences to contend with both in my childhood and from it. But I would not trade the bad experiences that happened to me, through nobody's fault, because each has made me who I am. And despite all my psychic bumps, bruises and missteps, I can honestly say that I feel proud of the person I have become and grateful for my parents' and my older siblings' loving roles in shaping me.

Do I miss my father? Of course, as I also miss my mother and her wise counsel. But I sometimes wonder if I was spared by Daddy's dying before my mildly stormy adolescence, so that both my love and admiration of him were preserved unambivalently. I'll never know. But I do know that my parents and their influence are with me daily. And I eagerly await reconnecting with them and my two dead sisters someday.

Like all immigrants, my parents' people faced hardships in coming to this country. And unlike some, they left a land where living conditions were hard for the vast majority of the year, due to the climate and the rugged terrain of Scandinavia. Since so much of the region is above the Arctic Circle, when the sun sets in November it does not return for months. In addition, the cold can be life threatening; people can die if outside unprotected in a blizzard at below-zero temperatures. Both of my parents' people emigrated to an area of the United States that reminded them of home where they could resume their familiar occupation of farming. They settled in Minnesota, where the weather was bone-chilling cold and the farming was hard. These people truly were pioneers, adventurers, despite great hardship. I, too, am an explorer; only I am exploring psychological hardship, in an effort to provide others with a map to this bleak and sometimes treacherous territory. With this map, I hope to help others in the same boat to identify the source of their pain and to take steps to resolve it. That is the purpose of this book.

2

Father Loss and Father Hunger

[A]nd still an everlasting funeral marches
'round your heart. . . .
Your justice would freeze beer!

—Arthur Miller
The Crucible

A lack of contact with and knowledge of their father leaves children with a gaping hole in their soul, best described as "father hunger." This natural longing, if left unfulfilled, too often dooms people to relentless personal and professional dead ends in an effort to fill that hole. This usually shows up in different ways that seem unrelated to father loss: food to fill the hole; workaholism in an attempt to run away from the hole; alcoholism or drug abuse to deaden the ache from it; depression from the pain of it; the thrill of sexual promiscuity to distract from the throbbing

19

hurt of it; or violence to act it out or to seal it over. Some people may manifest their pain in a revolving door of relationships because of their unconscious promise to never let anyone close enough to risk being hurt like that again.

That is, unless their father hunger is addressed directly and resolved. And even then, it casts a long shadow that people have to manage throughout their lives.

How to Tell Whether You Experience Father Hunger

Sometimes, the hole a father's absence creates is obvious, such as when there is no father to give a woman away at her wedding or to lead a Boy Scout troop. However, too often, father hunger masquerades as something else. And unfortunately, too often mental health professionals focus their treatment on that something else, labeling the problem addiction, codependency, depression, marital dysfunction, conduct disorder or any other diagnostic label du jour. And, obviously, if something is not accurately diagnosed, it is not treated. Thus, readers may find themselves on their own in doing the detective work required to determine whether they suffer from father hunger, even if they are currently seeing a mental health professional.

To help you figure out whether father hunger could be an issue for you or for someone you know, ask yourself the following questions. And don't forget to talk to yourself about them in your journal, either by answering each question or by taking a minute to make some general observations about your answers.

ACTION EXERCISE

Are you:

- fearful of depending on or getting too involved with people?
- untrusting of men?
- desperate to be taken care of?
- fearful of being viewed as needy?
- fearful of commitment?
- apathetic about commitment?
- a caretaker?
- a "control freak"?
- codependent - dependent?
- too fearful of being abandoned?
- a sex and love addict?
- chronically busy and overscheduled?
- afraid of being alone?
- chemically dependent or with someone who is?
- confused about what is expected behavior for men?
- confused about how to relate to men?
- afraid of men?
- frightened of responsibility?
- overresponsible?
- a loner?
- fearful of offending even strangers whom you will never see again?
- self-destructive?
- fearful of trying anything new?
- always around people so you don't have to be alone?
- overprotective with your children at their expense and at the expense of your primary relationship?

Do you feel:
- excessively worried about the future or the unknown?
- incompetent?
- chronic separation anxiety?
- low self-esteem?
- worthless?
- never good enough to measure up?
- detached from people, even and especially those you need the most?
- alienated from yourself?
- nothing because you stonewall your emotions?
- angry for no apparent reason?
- angry much of the time?
- at fault whenever anything goes wrong?
- guilty whether you have done something wrong or not?
- physically sick frequently?
- excessively worried about losing those closest to you?
- helpless?
- deprived and think you deserve to be?
- deprived and angry about it?
- a vague sense that something is missing or wrong, but you can't identify what?
- depressed for no apparent or "good" reason?

Do you think:
- it's safest to believe that it's you against the world?
- the past is in the past?
- there's no sense crying over spilled milk?
- no one can ever be counted on to stay with you?
- no one is there for you emotionally?
- everything you do has to be perfect?
- your children have to be perfect?

- your appearance has to be perfect?
- you are—or at least should be—the center of the universe?
- men are jerks?
- women are jerks?
- that people are to be loved and then left, before they leave you?
- becoming genuinely attached to people is too dangerous to risk?
- love should be hoarded?
- that you inevitably and eventually will be abandoned?
- sex equals intimacy?
- you are nothing without a mate?
- "needy" or "childlike" are dirty words?

Do you do:
- anything for love?
- everything to excess?
- things that you "know better" than to do, such as overeating, drinking too much, compulsive shopping or gambling, or going back to abusive relationships?
- nothing controversial, for fear of making a mistake or that people won't like you?
- compulsive sexual acts to prove that you are man enough or to keep a man?
- anything to create chaos, so you don't have to feel your emotions?
- excessively masculine or feminine activities?
- nothing that is risky, for fear of making a mistake?
- anything to cover up your needs?
- unfaithful, secretive acts?
- anything to deny responsibility, especially when something goes wrong?
- little to invest in relationships?

Answering one or even a few of these questions affirmatively does not prove that you experience father hunger. Some of these thoughts, feelings and personal attributes can result from other contributors. However, from my personal and clinical experience, answering yes to the majority of these questions is certainly cause to explore the issue further, to see whether or how you have been affected by the kind and quality of relationship you have or didn't have with your father.

Melanie: "Why Wasn't I Good Enough for Him to Stay?"

As we have already learned, many children from disrupted families have a hard time achieving intimacy. Although the specific reasons vary from person to person, in Melanie's case, she had concluded as a toddler that if she wasn't good enough for her daddy to stay, then surely no man could really love her. This, of course, made getting close to her husband virtually impossible because her unconscious reasoning went, *If I open myself up to him, then he'll see how inadequate I am, and he, too, will leave. So I'll stay behind my nice, safe wall.*

Melanie was a thirty-three-year-old homemaker when I met her and Anthony, who was fifteen years her senior and a highly responsible senior executive. By the time she and her husband came to therapy, he was furious about continually bashing his head into the brick wall of her defenses. And she was increasingly fearful that if she showed him the real Melanie, he'd be repulsed and leave. So she frantically added more and more bricks to her self-protective wall. Teetering on the brink of divorce, they desperately sought therapy to either end this destructive cycle or to sanely end their mutually damaging marriage.

Initially both were adamant that the marriage—but mostly the other person—was the root of their problems. As I listened to their stories, I became convinced that the beginning of their marital impasse occurred long before they ever met. It began thirty years before, when Melanie's father abandoned her. Though it took us considerable time to work up to those issues, they in fact were the bull's-eye for helping Melanie learn to value herself Melanie's renewed self-esteem, in turn, was largely responsible for saving their marriage.

Melanie's parents divorced when she was three years old, finally ending a marriage riddled with her mother's extra-marital affairs and embroidered by great emotional distance between the couple. Their last gasp was a custody fight over Melanie, which the father lost. Then, apparently believing he was doing the best for her, and probably because of his anger at her mother, Melanie's birth father relinquished her for adoption to the man the mother hastily married. After that, the father simply vanished. As more marriages with children end in divorce, our society will be seeing increasing numbers of these adoptions.

As if her father's abandoning her were not harmful enough, Melanie then used the self-centered and illogical logic that children frequently use to explain what they don't understand, which I will discuss in greater detail in the next chapter. Children's thought processes cause them to think concretely and to blame themselves for anything that goes wrong in their world. Melanie realizes now that she tried mightily to distract her parents from their marital issues and to keep them together. But when this effort failed, she felt *she* had failed.

Then, adding insult to injury, she silently explained her father's sudden disappearance as being further evidence that she truly was not good enough for anyone to love.

Thirty years later, she continued to act on this garbled conclusion that she had reached as a toddler and was "proving" it in her marriage and in her parenting. When her daughter turned three years old, Melanie's old wounds of low self-worth, feeling unlovable, and doubting herself surfaced and began aching with staggering intensity. Totally outside her awareness, these messages—relics from her past—were running her life.

For a long time, Anthony remained steadfast and devoted to her and to the marriage. But as the storm clouds became more ominous, he became increasingly weary of being pushed away by her painful but protective shield of self-loathing and self-doubt. Of course, Anthony had his part in their marital problems, which he worked on diligently. He had learned in his family to be hypercritical of himself and everyone else, which of course, was a "perfect" and perfectly horrible combination with Melanie. His judgments "helped" Melanie continue her own internal critique while allowing her to justify her increasingly expert mental masonry.

As is typical of people with unresolved issues, their marriage was a toxic but highly complementary match, and the initial stages of their therapy involved stopping this mutually created destructive cycle. Anthony needed to learn the fuel for his criticality and to stop it. But Melanie's work was much more emotionally precarious. When she grasped the role her childhood experiences played in her current difficulties, she finally took hold of her situation. Melanie somewhat reluctantly agreed to seek out her birth father. Until she faced the childish, distorted conclusions she had made about his absence and resolved her feelings by finally facing her father, all manner of irrational feelings and fears would drive her life. She had been unable to resolve them by years of "armchairing" discussions with her father in therapy. She finally acknowledged that she had to meet him. Because of her understandable fears of rejection, contacting him took enormous courage on her part, much support on Anthony's part and increasing insight as a result of our work. But doing so finally freed her and Anthony to live their life in the present, rather than trapped in the past.

Here's one comment she made in the course of the many weeks it took us to prepare her for their first encounter in thirty years:

> **Melanie:** I've spent my whole life trying to get back to where everything was all right. . . . I realize now that I've been preparing my whole life to meet my dad, trying to be good enough so that he would finally love me.

Profound, elegantly simple words. They speak of years of buried thoughts, hopes, wishes and fears that, though submerged, affected every area of her life. As a child and an adolescent, she had been a loner. She isolated herself further at boarding school so she could get straight A's. Though somewhat plain, she aspired to be a model and felt devastated when she didn't succeed. All of this, she realized thirty years later, had been in hopes of someday earning the approval of her phantom father.

When she and Anthony journeyed to the father's home in the next state, Melanie finally could ask him why he left her. And she finally could hear that it was not that he did not love her; he believed what he was doing was best for her. She also at last could hear that she had done nothing to provoke him to leave and could have done nothing to stop it. Of course, her adult, rational side knew all these things. But it was important to get these answers straight from the horse's mouth and at a feeling level. Then the answers to her haunting questions were no longer hypothetical or figments of her imagination.

Once she had these answers, she gradually began to gain the strength required to be genuinely vulnerable with Anthony. No longer plagued by the self-doubt that convinced her she was not good enough, she began to take charge of her own life. It was as if, by receiving her father's praise, she could see herself as worthy enough to be loved as a woman and a human being. To Anthony's delight, she began to meet him as an equal, instead of as an ashamed, naughty little girl hiding from a parent.

ACTION EXERCISE

Tracing Your Father's Imprint on Your Life

Settle back in your chair for a few moments and ponder the following questions:

- What is the most positive childhood experience you remember having with your father?
- With a male of any age?
- What is the most negative experience you remember having with your father in childhood?
- Which type of experience was harder to retrieve?
- Which type was easier?

- Which type of memory brought the strongest feelings?
- Which type of experience influenced you the most?
- How do these experiences prompt you to react to men?
- If you are a man, how do these experiences affect how you see yourself as a human being?
- As a man?
- As a father?
- How do they affect what you expect from and will give to relationships?
- How do they affect what you expect out of yourself in relationships?
- Out of life?
- If you are a woman, how do these experiences affect how you see yourself as a human being?
- As a woman?
- How do they affect what you expect from and will give to relationships?
- What you expect out of yourself in relationships?
- Out of life?

Now you may want to write in your journal the thoughts these questions spurred.

Of course, many of your thoughts, behaviors and feelings can come from multiple sources. However, if father absence is the core issue, your responses are likely rooted in it. *A father's emotional or literal absence both comes from and creates family dysfunction.* In turn, as will be discussed in the next chapter, this family dysfunction jeopardizes the healthy development of all the individuals in it. For example, a father is present but not really there if he is a practicing addict. His addiction both *creates* family dysfunction and *reflects* it. Or the father may come home from work faithfully every night, but if he is abusive when he is there, his children learn to stay away from him emotionally and literally in order to protect themselves from his wrath. Thus, his abusive behavior both *creates* dysfunction and *reflects* it, as the family organizes around it. This is true for the family as a whole and for the individuals in it.

As Melanie's case illustrates your father and your relationship with him provide a blueprint for how you see yourself. Second, the relationship you have or had with your father, for good or for ill, will have a major influence on how you handle the rest of your relationships. It acts as a template for what you expect and consider normal in relationships—even if those expectations repeatedly lead to disastrous outcomes. If you are a female, it unconsciously shapes what you expect in your intimate relationships and your view of your competence and your femininity. And if you are a male, it will determine whether you feel man enough to love a woman, to be a dad to your own kids and to compete in the world of grown-ups. I will discuss these influences in depth in chapter 5. And third, when you experience a loss as significant as the loss of your father, it has a profound and significant impact on your individual and relationship functioning.

What Sociologists Say About the Importance of Fathers

You may be wondering why father loss is special and what distinguishes it from other types of family dysfunction. More and more, contemporary sociologists are documenting what I experienced personally and see clinically. David Blankenhorn, founder and president of the Institute for American Values, wrote about the current trend of fatherlessness and the personal and societal nightmare it is creating. He stated:

Tonight, about 40 percent of American children will go to sleep in homes in which their fathers do not live. Before they reach the age of eighteen, more than half of our nation's children are likely to spend at least a significant portion of their childhoods living apart from their fathers. Never before in this country have so many children been voluntarily abandoned by their fathers. Never before have so many children grown up without knowing what it means to have a father. *Fatherlessness is the most harmful demographic trend of this generation. It is the leading cause of declining child well-being in our society.* [Emphasis added.] It is also the engine driving our most urgent social problems. . . . If this trend continues, fatherlessness is likely to change the shape of our society.[1]

Another prominent sociologist, David Popenoe of Rutgers University, cochair of the Council on Families, also wrote about the alarming societal drift toward viewing fathers as more and more superfluous to family life. He stated simply, "The evidence is strong: . . . involved fathers are indispensable for the good of children and society; and our growing national fatherlessness is a disaster in the making."[2] Barbara Defoe Whitehead also wrote of the consequences of fatherlessness that I have seen in my office for years. She stated, "research shows that many children from [father-absent] families have a harder time achieving intimacy in a relationship, forming a stable relationship or even holding a steady job."[3]

Many adults believe and act as if a child's relationship with their father is superfluous or a luxury. They don't realize the adverse effects their beliefs have on their child. Nor do they appear to grasp that a father's importance paradoxically increases when he is absent. Each parent makes a unique and unrepeatable contribution to children. Although other people can try to fulfill the parental role, no one else can adequately compensate. While their efforts undoubtedly help, like Band-Aids do for cut fingers, they provide only temporary relief for the ailment and not a cure for the disease. Substitute fathers simply are not the same as the genuine article.

My comments are not intended to be an indictment of customs that are becoming common as this century and millennium come to a close. Rather, I hope that the information I've provided can prevent unnecessary damage done to children by disposable dads and unaware moms. I hope to prevent the creation of more father hunger and to help you repair the damage that already may have been done unknowingly.

Now that you may have begun to wonder whether you or someone you know suffers from father hunger, in the next two chapters, we will consider the incubating conditions that create it.

References

1. David Blankenhorn, *Fatherless America: Confronting Our Most Urgent Social Problem* (New York: Basic Books, 1995), 1.

2. David Popenoe, *Life Without Father* (New York: Free Press, 1996), 2.

3. Barbara Defoe Whitehead, "Dan Quayle Was Right," *Atlantic Monthly,* April 1993: 55.

3 Father Absence and Child Development

*When I was a child,
I spoke as a child, I understood as
a child, I thought as a child: but when
I became an adult, I put away
childish things.*

—1 Cor. 13:11

As my own story illustrates, father hunger from any one source is difficult enough for children to manage. But many people suffer the agony of multiple sources with which they must cope. Cara is one such young woman. Her hunger for her traditional, adoptive father and for the birth father she never knew interacted with her own immature thought processes and her family's difficulty in moving through the developmental passage of divorce. This crippled her emotionally and left her individual psychological growth severely compromised.

Cara: "It's All My Fault, Isn't It?"

Every therapist can reminisce about unforgettable clients. I met Cara and her family fifteen years ago, and they fall into that category. Their case is classic in more ways than one. It both reinforces and illustrates this book's central concepts. It exemplifies what often happens when children are left on their own to cope with and understand trauma. Their naturally immature thought processes compound the damage already inherent in dysfunctional family dynamics and in the dynamics that both create and result from a father's absence.

Cara was fourteen years old at the time I met the family. I learned in the first session that she was adopted in infancy by two very attractive parents who appeared to her to be successful at everything they attempted. When Cara's mom called for an appointment, I recognized the family's name because her dad was a prominent physician in the city and his name was a household word. I, unfortunately, was not surprised when her dad did not show up for the initial appointment or for many following it. I also learned in the first session that because her dad had cronies in the legal profession who pulled strings, the parents were divorced eleven days from their first discussion of her mom's wish to improve their communication. Still in shock, Cara's mom moved out but returned home daily to resume her former homemaker role. This often included sitting at her place at the table and sleeping with her former husband in their bed. She must have felt as if she had been fired, and pretending it wasn't so was her golden parachute! Thus, the family entered a twilight zone created by the parents being neither married nor (emotionally) divorced. Even though four years had passed when I met them, they all were living in suspended animation, in a state of shock. It was as though no one had torn off any calendar pages as they hung in their emotional time warp.

Since Cara, an only child, was clearly out of control, her mom's worry and embarrassment were virtually palpable when mother and daughter settled next to each other uneasily on my couch like crows perched on a wire on a windy day.

Mom began by describing how she had taken Cara to two other individually oriented counselors, to no avail. Cara remained impervious to everyone's entreaties, bribes and tirades, messing up with even more severe consequences. Despite Cara's obvious problems, I gently but firmly insisted that the spotlight be gradually taken off her, as a paradoxical way to solve her problems. My training, belief and experience suggest that a child's dysfunction is most efficiently and effectively addressed when seen in the context of the whole family. Then, everyone can help fix the problem, together modifying all parts of the family system by each person changing within it. This allows for correction of the dysfunctional relationship dynamics that plague the family and stunt everyone's growth and development, while solving the problem that brought the family to therapy in the first place.

This led to my central hypothesis. Rather than viewing Cara as a problem child, I chose to view her acting out as a *marker* of her own and her family's unexpressed and unresolved grief which simultaneously and paradoxically *masked* that grief. With everyone focused on her misbehavior, there was no risk that any submerged feelings could surface. And yet, lack of appropriate attention to their emotions kept everyone stalled, unable to grieve and move on. This also kept Cara stuck in her frantic attempts to get her preoccupied and unavailable father's attention. Thus, Cara was trapped in the tyrant role while at the same time she sadly was her family's sacrificial lamb. While these hapless people clearly were not playing their rigid roles consciously or intentionally, they all were taking part in the family's dance to protect their predivorce status quo.

It is important to make a subtle but fundamental distinction. I am *not blaming* the parents or the family for Cara's problems, any more than I blamed Cara for her behavior. *Accountability is not the same as blame.* Rather, I am saying that her behavior was rooted in the natural grief process that all in her family were having trouble accomplishing. It was up to me to help them figure out where their process was logjammed and what would correct it, so that everyone could get on with life.

Not surprisingly, my approach was a tough sell. To the frightened and frazzled parents, Cara's behavior seemed extreme and ominous. I agreed. Mom, who was also Dad's mouthpiece, reported that they felt that Cara needed to learn to accept basic limits for her own good. Once again, I agreed. Not helping her learn this would leave big power in little hands, to everyone's detriment. It also would jeopardize Cara's getting along in the world. Already Cara was failing in school, due primarily to truancy. She had friends from a rough crowd. She was experimenting with drugs. She vacillated between being sullen and uncommunicative or openly hostile and defiant at home. She was a mess in the personal hygiene department, which appalled her two beautiful parents. She appeared to be doing everything that fourteen-year-old girls can do to act out, stopping just short of getting pregnant.

Cara's behavior was alarming to the mother and, she reported, to the father. And it must have been to Cara, too, because she never resisted our appointments. Still, I could not draw the attention of this attending physician father away from his patients long enough to attend to his own daughter. It was easy to see how Cara must have felt! Yet, I knew that I needed to enlist his participation in solving this family's problems and in Cara's life, or she would have to up the ante to compel his attention. The more he protested to me on the phone that the problem was Cara and that she, her mother and I could and should solve it, the more I stressed that his participation in the therapy, and ultimately in Cara's life, was essential.

Finally, Cara took matters into her own hands and got her dad into therapy. She stole his brand-new $75,000 Mercedes and drove it drunk with a carload of friends. That got her dad's attention! Although he usually arrived for sessions a few minutes late and breathless from bounding up the three flights of stairs to my office, he was now finally on board.

The initial stages of our work involved standard family therapy interventions that the pioneer Salvador Minuchin taught. I helped the parents learn appropriate behavior control strategies, how to be a functional united front and how to take back the power from their child. Even though I was focusing on Cara's behavior, I knew this work had to be done first, and I was viewing it in context. Not doing this would allow Cara to continue to provide a smoke screen behind which she and the family could hide, all the while sacrificing herself. But I also knew that unless the dysfunctional family dynamics that were fueling her acting out were addressed, she could not afford to straighten up. Thus, I waited for the "therapeutic moment" to examine aloud the family's emotional and communication processes that propelled Cara's behavior.

That opportunity finally came. The parents were gaining confidence in working together to manage Cara, and she was beginning to change in response. Gingerly, I asked, "So, Cara, what's your understanding of why your parents got divorced?" Without a moment's hesitation, her response was clear: "Because I didn't clean my room."

Before I could help the family work with that stark statement, something even more fascinating happened. Her mom shrieked, "Oh my God! We're divorced!" In a very real way, because information can take an eternity to travel from head to gut, she had just received the news. She then started to sob. Almost immediately, her daughter joined her. Relieved, I turned to her dad to see his response. I was encouraged to find that this traditional father and man's man scarcely could contain the tears rimming his eyes. But he tried mightily as, in a classic Freudian slip, he amusingly and absentmindedly sat tearing my business card into tiny shreds. Although I made no comment on this action, I surmised that it was in acknowledgment of his chagrin at seeing the grieving no one had done and now must do, and at facing his contribution to Cara's misery.

Children Reason Differently

Children's reasoning processes compound the impact of their father's abandonment. Understanding this may help you capture and name some elusive dimensions of your own childhood. It also may help parents take steps to prevent damage that is not already inherent in certain situations for their children. It will provide a context for understanding the aftershocks created by the earthquake of a father's unavailability, which are heightened as children struggle to make sense of their loss and his abandonment.

Children think qualitatively differently from adults. The Swiss psychologist Jean Piaget observed this when, watching his daughter, he became curious about the way children think.[1] He came up with two conclusions that have particular relevance to father loss. First, he noticed that children engage in *concrete thinking*, in contrast to an adult's ability to think abstractly. This means that, while adults mentally can step back and question the reasonableness of their thoughts, children just think their thoughts in an immediate fashion and without introspection. For example, adults sometimes respond to children's request for attention with "in a minute," hoping to put off responding until a more opportune time. However, the next moment, children are back, pressing their demands for attention with even greater urgency because that "minute" is over. Rather than interpret this behavior as that of irksome children, perhaps a more accurate explanation is that, in children's concrete and literal minds, the adult can be expected to be available on the second request. An amusing illustration of children's garbled, concrete thinking is a drawing of an Easter story that a child brought home from Sunday school. It was of a man in an airplane, whom the child proudly announced was Pontius, the pilot, on the flight to Egypt.

Because of children's concrete thinking, a father's emotional or literal desertion likely will have a powerfully different impact on them than it would have on adults. The explanation for a father's abandonment of his child in the typical young person's mind is simple: He did not stay because I must have done something bad to make him go away, as both Cara's and Melanie's stories illustrate. Adults, who presumably are capable of abstract thinking, can reason that children have nothing to do with fathers' choices. But children, who do not become capable of abstract thinking until they approach adolescence, are stuck thinking their first thought. And then, what becomes even more psychologically precarious is that too often, children extrapolate even further on their conclusion. They determine that if their parent—who is supposed to love them no matter what—leaves, no one else can be counted on to stay. And further, they often figure that this probably means they aren't lovable or worthy of being loved anyway. These conclusions usually remain lodged deep in their minds, unless some adult, preferably the father, succeeds in reassuring them otherwise.

These sorts of explanations can be problematic enough for the children who talk about their conclusions. At least then they can receive reassurance, corrective information and help from adults to see the father's behavior in a less personalized, more accurate way. Tragically and all too often, however, children are left on their own to make sense of their experience. And even when they would not need to sort it out alone because there are emotionally available adults, their reasoning seems perfectly logical to them, so few even bring it up. This is true especially if they feel shame about the inferences they have drawn. The damaging conclusions that children naturally tend to make are often questioned by adults only when these youngsters' behavior manifests disastrous effects, as was the case with Cara. And by the time her thought process finally came to light, much damage already had been done. The belief that she was unlovable and unworthy already had become deeply ingrained in her psyche and was difficult to modify.

Piaget observed that children do not develop the ability to begin thinking abstractly until somewhere between ages eleven and sixteen.[2] Only then have children developed the cognitive hardware that allows them to question their own thoughts and to see the implications of their conclusions. Only then do they have the ability to grasp the vicissitudes of their father's absence. Sadly, Piaget concluded that a surprising number of individuals never learn abstract thought at all. Those people are left to cope with an event as momentous as a father's absence with the reasoning of a child, regardless of their chronological age. However, as we will see throughout this book, once the vagaries of their thought process come to light, the grooves in their psyche etched by their childhood reasoning can be modified, even though doing so is a slow, gradual process.

Piaget's second conclusion about children's thought processes that is particularly relevant to father loss deals with *egocentrism*. Children learn from birth to be highly self-centered creatures. Most children naturally learn that when they signal, their needs can be satisfied. They smile and coo, and people smile and talk back. They wet themselves, and someone comes with a clean, dry diaper. They howl, and they get fed. From this, they learn to feel very powerful and even the center of the universe. In fact, as another great theorist of child development, Margaret Mahler, and her colleagues remind us, the primary developmental task for children in the first six months of life is learning to distinguish self from all-powerful mother, from whom initially they can make no distinction.[3] Children are mother, and mother is children. It is a parent's primary job to socialize children away from their egocentrism so that they no longer see themselves as the center of the universe. As they do, gradually children learn to acknowledge the needs and importance of others.

Egocentrism is relevant to father loss because if children see themselves as all-powerful and the center of the universe, then they typically reason that if something goes wrong in their universe, it must be their fault. Children who have already been damaged by their life experiences and their egocentric conclusions about them accept responsibility for nothing. This is how a father's absence, which clearly is an adult choice and responsibility in all instances except death, becomes transmuted in a child's mind into it being the child's own fault. This belief, too, needs to be clarified so it can be modified. At the end of this chapter are some exercises to help readers uncover any residual childish thoughts they still may harbor.

A Father's Abandonment Affects a Child's Ego Development

The whole of a child's identity development is affected when a father voluntarily absents himself. The best way for children to learn who they are is to know where they came from. Even if they do not particularly like what they know, humans experience a basic drive to know where they fit, to whom they belong and who their people are. This information then can form both a platform and a springboard for going out into the world to explore what they will become. Conversely, when they do not possess such firsthand knowledge of their roots, no matter how distressing that knowledge is, they are likely to experience profound confusion about who they are and whether they matter. Most either yearn for this knowledge or seal it off with great effort and at great cost. An eleven-year-old client of mine, relinquished for adoption in infancy, wept bitter tears about never knowing her birth parents. Wishing to see them just once, she moaned, "I just want to know if that's where I get my brown eyes. And I want to know if they're good artists, too." Her lack of knowledge of them created an aching void that her devoted adoptive parents simply could not fill, try as they might. Only direct and personal knowledge about her birth parents could relieve the ambiguity, and tragically for her, that information was sealed in closed adoption files.

For better or worse, parents provide the lion's share of the supplies that children need and use to grow into loving and productive human beings. This is not to say that others cannot infuse people with some provisions of their own. Many can vouch for their psychological lives being saved by a grandparent, neighbor, teacher, minister, older sibling or even a spouse who reached out. But even then, when a father remains aloof, unavailable or uninvolved, some part of them is likely to conclude that this is because they are unworthy of involvement. This part also usually despairs of ever being truly loved, even with much information to the contrary. Because the grooves etched in psyches by early experiences are deep, they never totally disappear. However, they can be managed more effectively once the person gains knowledge and emotional closure.

Although volumes could be and have been written about children's need for their parents, perhaps the nugget is this. It seems possible for children to risk and even to revel in standing alone, as long as three circumstances are present. First, if it is children, not parents, who initiate the separation that inevitably follows healthy individuation. Second, if parents remain reliably available to children, even in their physical absence. Third, if children can go back to their parents for emotional pit stops when they need to do so. When each of these conditions is present, children can feel safe and even gain strength by being apart from parents.

However, it is another matter when a father leaves his children, even if his absence is not his choice, such as is the case with natural death. When fathers leave instead of the reverse, children generally feel discarded, expelled and unlovable. This especially goes for abusive, addicted or traditional fathers living in the home but who might as well occupy the outer rings of Saturn. And even in the case of abandonment by natural causes, children are left with a fierce hunger that is difficult for them or for anyone who loves them to satisfy. Thus, it is easy to see how an absent father leaves children with a voracious appetite, thereby ironically *increasing* his importance in many ways.

In sum, there is little dispute among child development experts about the fact that parental abandonment of children has a profound and disruptive impact on their lives. This and the trauma their absence leaves in its wake have the capacity and even the tendency to derail a child's emotional and social development.

Family Development: Platform and Ceiling

Just as Piaget concluded that there is an underlying order to individuals' development, the early work of Elizabeth Carter and Monica McGoldrick identified the developmental tasks with which all families must successfully grapple.[4] Developmental tasks are those basic processes that individuals and families must complete in order for progression to the next stage to take place. The completion of these developmental tasks is important, regardless of the age of family members. Whether a couple marries at twenty years old or at forty years old, successful completion of the first family developmental task of forming their own family hinges on two people who can stand on their own, apart from their families of origin. While arguably it is easier for a forty-year-old to have completed this task than someone much younger, it is essential nonetheless. In turn, a family's successful completion of each subsequent developmental step will be impeded without their having attained the previous one.

If the primary function of the family is to support the development of the individuals in it, then successful achievement of individual developmental tasks is dependent on and contributes to the effective accomplishment of each family developmental transition. Thus, *family and individual development are interlocking and highly interdependent.* Each is not possible without the other.

As we saw with Cara, people often develop emotional, physical or behavioral symptoms that both prevent their progression to the next stage and mark their difficulty. Most likely, this is because their family's typical communication patterns do not promote or even permit the emotional work required to make this shift. This can be true with any family. But families with a history of chronic, unresolved loss are especially susceptible to degrees of rigidity that prevent the adequate expression of grief. So yet another loss stacks up behind the original loss, which

sometimes occurred generations ago and long since has passed
into the family's collective unconscious.

Is it possible for one family member to resolve a loss if the
rest of the family resists? The answer is a cautious yes. The
individual who faces what the rest of the family is attempting
to deny can expect to encounter disapproval and even censure.
Thus, moving toward one's own healing needs to be planned
and carried out carefully. Individuals who come from
extremely rigid families may not want to begin this work
without the help of a therapist who understands how families
of origin function to act as a coach or shaman. This way, they
will not be going into the lion's den alone.

Janine: When Individuals Need What Their Family Cannot Provide

Janine, a twenty-four-year-old university student of mine in
a family studies course, was a single mother. Without realizing it, she illustrated the interaction between individual and
family development. This is a brief excerpt from a weekly
reflection paper that she wrote after a class discussion on how
early attachment experiences influence adult relationships.

> This past week had a profound effect on me. When we talked
> about anxious/ambivalent relationships in class, I knew that it
> perfectly fit me. I told my mom about the theory, and she said
> she could see why I might be leaning towards being ambiva-
> lent. My father died when I was three, and even when he was
> alive, he was mostly in Vietnam. (He was a major in the Air
> Force.) Then my mom's second husband died also. After that,
> my mom really turned into a heavy drinker, and I saw a lot of

men come and go in her life. How could that *not* have an impact on me?

Here Janine only began to scratch the surface of how her father's absence became a blueprint for her relationships. Her difficulty in dealing appropriately with her father and step-father's deaths was shaped by her mother's problems with the sudden and untimely deaths of two husbands. This arrested the development of Janine, her mother and their family. Each of the deaths and her mother's attempt to drown her sorrows with booze rather than resolve them established the ceiling beyond which Janine was unable to progress.

If the heads of a family cannot accomplish a developmental task, their individual deficit will create a family impasse. This in turn will affect their children's development. For Janine, this resulted in her inability to learn to trust anyone or to build a lasting relationship. Specifically, she had a son by a military man who was stationed several states away and saw her and their son only occasionally, despite her belief that he was her fiancé. Thus we also see how the developmental arrest in her family of origin spawned her own developmental arrest and, in turn, one in the nuclear family she was trying to create.

Family Rules—Covert Decrees

All families develop rules over time, and mine was no exception. As I have stated, I certainly sensed that I was not to grieve my father's loss openly, although this was not explicitly stated. Rules determine (explicitly or implicitly) emotions and behavior that are acceptable or unacceptable, and whether or how emotions are to be expressed. This is why the first few years of a marriage can be so stormy: Couples are in the process of developing a consensus about what works for both and about how to conduct their new family. The rules that develop from these tussles are rarely articulated because they seldom are known on a conscious level. Still, couples negotiate for consensus on rules embedded in issues like how to relate to in-laws and children; how to resolve conflict; priorities for spending money; and when, how, and how often to have sex.

Family rules are not necessarily bad. Once agreed to, however unconsciously, they serve as stabilizers and protectors of the family's equilibrium. This is because, however covertly, they stipulate the expectations that guide daily family life. Routines become predictable, and life becomes safe. Then there is an economy of effort. Everyone knows the parameters and can get on with living within them. To take a mundane example, ask yourself who usually starts the coffee in your household in the morning—or for that matter, at work. If yours is like many households, it is probably the same person whose job often was delegated without discussion of the matter.

However, sometimes rules can be suffocating. When a family is rigid and unyielding in its demands for conformity, there is a powerful and destructive push to maintain the status quo that develops, and both reinforces and derives from allegiance to the family's rules. As tyranny constricts individuals, it also denies the family the required flexibility for making normal developmental shifts and the multiple changes that day-to-day life can bring. Rigid families fight the reality that the only constant is change.

Rob: Real Men Don't Show Feelings

A high-tech salesman in his early fifties, Rob came to therapy because he could not let down his guard with his fiancée, even though he knew he needed and wanted to do so. Divorced for eight years, his fiancée had made it perfectly clear that he would lose her, too, if he could not open up. But he felt terrified, small and stuck, looking only at the floor as he lay out his dilemma, an odd incongruity for a gray-haired man in a pinstriped power suit.

His father was a career man in the navy throughout the boy's childhood. This meant he was deployed at sea for six months at a time at regular intervals. Although in the following excerpt Rob was unaware that he was articulating some of his family's cardinal rules, still this explained his understanding of his family's expectations. Placed in the context of father hunger, it also is an eloquent illustration of the combustible combination of growing up in a family with an absent father and a no-talk rule.

> **Rob:** *(With tears welling in his eyes)* When my father left for the first time, I guess I must've felt, "Don't share. Don't trust. Hide your feelings." Because my dad retired after twenty-five years of service, that meant he would've been gone for most of my formative years, when I was learning to build trust. This must've developed in me a wanting not to be left—a fear of being alone.

Because family rules are seldom articulated, Rob did not know consciously what he knew unconsciously. However, he nonetheless was dimly aware of his family's messages that prohibited expression of emotions. And although any family may develop counterproductive rules, those that govern or restrict the expression of emotion can be particularly repressive because the expression of feelings is essential to grieving any loss as well as to bonding with others. When emotions are prohibited, people are expected to give up who they are in the service of maintaining the family's fragile status quo. No doubt, Rob's family rules helped the parents not be reminded constantly of the father's imminent or actual absences, but they had devastating consequences for Rob.

I often tell my clients that people would be better off if their family had posted the rules on the refrigerator for all to see. But none does. Unfortunately, often the only way people know their family's rules is through breaking them. Then the sanctions usually are swift and can be severe. Just how severe the consequences are is a marker of the rigidity and precariousness of life in a given family.

ACTION EXERCISE

Tracing the Reverberations of Your Father's Unavailability

I suggest this exercise to help you identify the chain reaction of thoughts, feelings and conclusions you may have reached as a child because of your father's absence. The goal is to offer you a chance to become aware of any childish concrete thinking and egocentric conclusions you may have employed to comprehend and to manage your father's unavailability. Articulating these will clarify what you attempted to do to establish the illusion of control of events that, in reality, were out of your control.

To complete the exercise, fill in whatever thoughts that come up from reading "My Father Was Not Available to Me," located at the end of this chapter. Write the first thought that springs from the one before, and so on. Think of this as brainstorming, so the same rules apply. Do not judge, evaluate or censor thoughts, but simply record them, letting your mind wander as you make a record of your mental chain reaction.

When you feel satisfied that you have teased out all your thoughts and feelings, draw a line under the last answer and ask yourself to total the sum of your answers.

Then, employ your adult reasoning ability. That is, step back and reflect on what you have written. It may help to ask yourself the following questions: What do I notice? How accurate is it when I apply adult reasoning? If my child had concluded what I did, how would I help that child? How can I help myself with this now?

Aaron: "I'm Zip!"

Aaron was a forty-five-year-old accountant who was a senior partner in a large and very successful accounting firm. When Serena, his wife of fifteen years, became severely depressed after learning she was infertile, her physician referred her for therapy. When I said I wanted her husband to join us, she was surprised but said that he had requested that. Much to her surprise and delight, we began a course of marital treatment.

As they sat opposite each other chatting stiffly, it was apparent that the couple obviously had a pleasant and cordial relationship. But I also sensed an emotional distance between them. In an attempt to help them bridge that gap, I probed to understand what caused it. For Aaron's part, he usually was away from home virtually all of his waking hours. Either he was at work, exercising or playing thirty-six holes of golf in one day with his buddies. Seldom did the couple do anything together, which Serena not surprisingly experienced as rejection and a message that she was not good enough. Depressing for any spouse, it was compounded because this meant that he was leaving his wife on her own to cope with their infertility and her depression. Unbeknownst to her, Aaron's inattentiveness and unavailability to her when she needed him set off echoes of the loss of her father. Her parents had divorced when she was seven years old, and she never saw her father again. All of these relics from her past merged with the voids in her current situation to produce her depression. But the concrete reasoning she employed as a child to comprehend the incomprehensible made Aaron's virtually constant absences even worse. Because of her child-hood experiences, Aaron's behavior was further "proof" that she was not worthy of being loved by a man. It also was a crushing reminder of a barrage of unresolved emotions that she numbed out by her depression.

However, understanding the contributors to Aaron's apparent insensitivity to a woman he obviously loved was a bit subtler. Although Aaron initially reported growing up in a happy home with his large extended family, he gradually came to understand that he was a lonely child. He was an only child of a traditional father, also an accountant, who was nearly always at work. When he was home, Dad was exhausted and isolated himself from everyone, which Aaron realized he interpreted as Dad's preference to be at work. This was compounded by Aaron's learning disability that convinced the boy he was stupid and caused him to isolate himself defensively from parents and peers. It also required expensive tutors who, in turn, kept the father at work and caused the son to feel guilty about the cost and inconvenience.

One day as we were musing on Aaron's life with his father and on how much Aaron was like him, I asked him to complete the exercise. Here are his responses.

AARON'S ACTION EXFRCISE

My Dad Was Not Available to Me

He worked hard.

He was always busy.

When he came home, he was tired.

I was a bother because I needed tutors and that was expensive.

If he had to do something with me, I was a bother.

When he did something special with me, my mom pushed him to do it.

He'd rather be doing something else because I was not important.

Spending time with me was not important.

I'm zip!

When I asked Aaron what all of this added up to, he replied, "There's nothing really to add up! It'd be a negative number." When I asked how seeing all this made him feel, he said what children of typical traditional fathers generally experience: "I guess it hurts because I think I was important to my dad and still am. But I guess it hurts because I just didn't feel it."

People can become stuck and languish in emotional limbo for a lifetime. However, that situation does not have to be. It is the purpose of this book to help people identify and resolve their father loss.

It truly is never too late to have a good childhood. That is, if people face their losses and rework them at the source.

ACTION EXERCISE

My Father Was Not Available to Me

References

1. Jean Piaget, *The Moral Judgment of the Child* (1932; reprint, Glencoe, Ill.: Free Press, 1948), 35.

2. Ibid.

3. Margaret Mahler, Fred Pine, and Anni Bergman, *The Psychological Birth of the Human Infant* (New York: Basic Books, 1975), 45.

4. Elizabeth Carter and Monica McGoldrick, eds., *The Family Life Cycle: A Framework for Family Therapy* (New York: Gardner, 1980), 20.

4 Seven Sources of Father Hunger

Give sorrow words.
The grief that does not speak
Whispers the o'erfraught heart
and bids it break.

—William Shakespeare
Macbeth

All father hunger springs from one main source: desertion. A father's abdication may be total or emotional or what the individual *experiences* as desertion. There are seven specific causes of father loss: death, divorce, single mothering, adoption, addiction, abuse and traditional fathering. The common element with all but one is the *father's choice* to absent himself. A father's death, unless it is a suicide, usually is experienced differently by a child because usually it is not the father's choice. This can insulate children from what likely would be their egocentric conclusion that his absence is somehow their fault, unless they get an idea into their head to the contrary. Still, death is abandonment, and therefore, it contains elements of desertion, absent the self-recrimination that usually accompanies other kinds of abandonment. Therefore, it usually does not carry the same emotional sting of his voluntary opting out of the child's life.

Oren: "What Did I Do?"

When Oren was six years old, his father dispatched him to catch his mother having sex with the man's best friend and business partner. Of course, the boy had no way to anticipate that the results of his detective work would be disastrous. He was merely doing what he had been told. The aftermath of Oren's discovery was havoc for the family. To add insult to injury, after the parents catapulted through a messy divorce, Oren never saw his birth father again until well into adulthood. This was only one brief and perfunctory visit, despite the man's living in a neighboring state.

Oren's mother soon married her lover. Oren tried to be a big boy and carry on as though nothing had happened. However, life with stepfather was rocky, even on their best days. Oren, who desperately wanted and needed a father, vacillated between polar opposite reactions. On the one hand, he tried hard to get his stepfather to fill the void left by his father, while on the other hand he rejected the man who appeared to have caused the family turmoil in the first place. For his part, the stepfather remained aloof, and by his own admission years later in my office, was unduly critical and demanding. Because he had no concept of reasonable expectations for children, he set his hopelessly high for Oren. For example, he expected Oren to assemble a car engine that the man had dismantled piece by piece. He was to do so totally by himself with no instruction—at age fourteen.

By the time Oren was nineteen, he had grown weary of the fierce and seemingly endless confrontations with his stepfather. So he fled, living in his car until he earned enough money to begin college and then hastily marrying the first coed who would have him.

Despite his enmity toward his stepfather, he managed to absorb the resourcefulness that the man apparently tried to teach him. Oren's professional life was filled with stunning success. Having completed three graduate degrees in unrelated fields, he owned a very lucrative consulting business when he began seeing me for counseling almost thirty years later. However, his personal life was a shambles. Married and divorced two times, he found his relationships broke up when he was caught having affairs. Each time, he became more fearful about trusting either himself or anyone else. So he developed an extreme version of the inability to be in or to maintain an intimate relationship: philandering. He literally would get out of bed with one woman and immediately begin hunting his next mark.

Although it might be easy to look at his behavior with women and find it disgusting, looked at through a different lens, his conduct made sense, as desperate and destructive as even he knew it was. Seeing his behavior in its proper historical context makes it more possible not to judge him or too readily condemn his conduct. For instance, fatherless boys often cope with their confusion about how to be a man by developing a facade of hypermasculinity. Men get messages from our culture that sexual prowess equals masculinity, manliness and, therefore, being man enough. With this binocular vision, it is easy to see the imprint left on him of his early sexualized experience and how that ultimately resulted in his having to figure out how to be a man without a reliable, trustworthy father as a male role model.

Death

Although certainly painful, a parent's death is often the easiest type of father loss for children to cope with, *if it is a death by natural causes.* This is paradoxical because death is final and allows no opportunity for having dad at piano recitals or athletic events. It is more bearable for several reasons. First and foremost, because death is no one's choice and because it's a part of life, children can be insulated from their egocentric tendencies to blame themselves. Second, the existence of socially sanctioned rituals helps. Support, compassion, cakes and tuna casseroles usually surround survivors. Third, since death is a finite end point, it helps everyone move on from there. This makes it easier to get closure when a father dies, in contrast to the other sources where there is perpetual lack of closure. Finally, even though there is naturally some wishing and fantasizing that the deceased person will return, because he is no longer seen, the unrequited love eventually ends or at least diminishes. This is in sharp contrast to divorce, for example, where even adult children of remarried parents often remain hostile to the stepmother out of loyalty to and protection of the prior family and out of their fantasies regarding eventual reunion. Still, death is abandonment and, therefore, it contains elements of desertion, absent the self-recrimination that usually accompanies the six other sources.

As I experienced it, death gets its power to cripple when families deliver the implicit or explicit decree that the loss is not to be discussed—or even felt. This is a particular risk for boys programmed by our culture that big boys don't cry. On top of these socialized messages, especially families with unresolved loss add, "Don't dwell on it," or "The past is in the past," or "There's no sense crying over spilled milk." These families are especially prone to exact loyalty to the rule that losses are to be kept just where they have always been: out of sight and out of mind.

This conspiracy of silence must be broken in order for people to resolve their loss and to heal. They need help and encouragement to name the loss, to grieve it, and then to make meaning of the person's life and death and their own in light of the loss, in order to move on emotionally. Without this, people are left to bury their loss underground. And if a child is involved with an adult who has experienced unresolved loss, this disowned loss often unconsciously spills over onto the child in numerous ways. Then, both child and parent will unwittingly become mired in its silent web.

Stan and Mitchell: High-Voltage Connection

Stan's disowned loss spilled over unknowingly onto his young son. Stan was a thirty-five-year-old enlisted military man when he, his wife Cheryl, their seven-year-old son and their four-year-old daughter, sought help to deal with Mitchell's nasty behavior. The parents were baffled about Mitchell's sudden meanness to his sister and his defiance at school. Mitchell even sadly described his own behavior as that of a "rotten" kid, expressing no particular pride in seeing himself that way. It was as though when Mitchell turned seven, someone plugged him in!

I began, to no avail, with standard family therapy interventions that emphasize helping parents and children modify their behavior. The intensity of Mitchell's acting out seemed to increase at the possibility that his protective behavior might be taken away. So I sought a historical explanation for Mitchell's behavior. This was the mother lode for this family's resolution of the pain that Mitchell unconsciously had been acting out for his father.

Cheryl had experienced a relatively uneventful childhood with no traumatic events. She'd always known that she was loved by both parents. Stan was not so fortunate. His father, an electrician, accidentally electrocuted himself on the job at age thirty-five, when Stan was seven years old. Because they came from an ethnic group that emphasized stoicism and repression of emotion, and because the rural culture in which the family lived strictly reinforced these values, the father's tragic death was never discussed with Stan. In fact, probably because his mother thought she was protecting a child too young to deal with death, Stan did not attend the funeral.

Once we identified the event that had blown Stan's emotional circuits, I had surprisingly little difficulty in convincing him that he needed to go back in his mind, heart and in reality, in order for everyone to be able to move forward. I urged him to make a sojourn back to the small Midwestern hometown in which the family lived when his father died. I encouraged him to talk with his father's friends and relatives to flesh out details of the man he scarcely remembered or knew. Knowing it would be extremely difficult to do, I even suggested that he drive down the country road where the accident happened. All of this culminated in a visit to the little country church where the funeral had taken place, followed by a trip to his father's grave to "talk" with him and to place flowers in his memory.

All of these actions gave him a qualitatively different ending to a painful and unresolved scenario. Cheryl's being there all the way helped tremendously. Finally, he could cry out and someone heard. And he literally could say good-bye, thereby putting the period at the end of a very long, lonely, dark sentence.

When Stan and Cheryl returned from their pilgrimage to the little town where his life was so drastically transformed, he had changed. And so had Mitchell. Both father and son expressed and exuded a sense of calm and peacefulness not usually experienced by both. Stan had closure at last, and Mitchell was unplugged. Finally, he could stop working overtime telegraphing and dissipating his father's sadness, which Mitchell had converted into restlessness and activity.

Divorce

The chance that a first marriage occurring today will end in divorce stands at 50 percent by some estimates, and as high as 60 percent by others. By contrast, in the middle of the past century, this number was around 5 percent. In the last three decades alone, the divorce rate has doubled or tripled, depending upon how one calculates.[1] At the same time, the percentage of children whose parents have divorced is increasing as this millennium comes to a close. That means that the odds of children today witnessing the divorce of their parents are much greater than they were even a generation ago.

Before we look at the impact of divorce on children, it is important to place it in the context of how divorce typically affects parents. Perhaps the single most significant and consistent research finding is that parents who divorce usually have a diminished capacity to parent, at least for a while. Because divorce is so traumatic for most people, even those who initiate it can experience multiple ripple effects. This family disruption creates a deep division between parents' interests and the interests of their children. Sadly and all too often, when children need their parents desperately, they instead experience a withdrawal of parental investment in their well-being. This happens because parents simultaneously are trying to lick their own wounds, cope with the massive changes inherent in divorce and restabilize themselves. Parental distraction and self-absorption are among the worst consequences for children because now the sacrifices, if there are any to be made, must come from the children. And yet, unfortunately, for children to succeed socially and psychologically even in the best of times in our increasingly complex culture, they must have strong and stable attachments to adults. For most, this need arises at a time when their parents are least able to fill it. Although divorce disrupts people's lives, it does not have to interfere with their connections. But too frequently it does.

Divorce can be a fertile breeding ground for father hunger, because the majority of children usually must live away from their father for many reasons. One is the prevalence of the "tender years" doctrine, which assumes that children need and belong to their mothers. Also, just as men's primary source of power in marriage was making money, women's was rearing children. Many fathers see marriage and children as a package deal, so if they are not involved in one, many have difficulty seeing themselves involved in the other. Perhaps this explains why many uninvolved fathers do not feel obligated to continue paying child support. In addition, fathers' socialization as males, which predisposes them *toward* productivity and being providers and *away from* relationships, can leave them not noticing, or denying, their and their children's emotional and relational needs. Still other fathers who have a rigid definition of a "real man" cannot square involved parenting with manly pursuits. This belief often is reinforced by their work culture, whether corporate or blue collar, as they experience or fear sanctions from too much time and attention spent on parenting. And still others simply do not realize their importance to children. Too often, both parents encourage what amounts to his divorcing the children because it is easier for the parents to not have to deal with each other. A mother in a recent divorce mediation I conducted said to the father, "Just give me ten-thousand dollars and the kids, and you'll never have to deal with any of us again!" Given the father's concern for his children despite his ineptitude as a parent, it was unlikely he would have accepted her offer. However, if he had, I would have provided both of them information she obviously did not have about the disastrous psychological consequences of their making such a choice.

Nevertheless, this is *not* to be taken as a suggestion that parents squabble over who is to be the primary caregiver. Rather, it is a strong suggestion that *both* parents work to ensure the ongoing, meaningful and consistent involvement of *both* parents in their children's lives. Unfortunately, this too infrequently happens, to everyone's and our society's detriment.

Andrew: Fathered by a Fatherless Son

Andrew, age twenty-nine when he came to therapy, realized that he would be chronically restless and unhappy if he did not get help. He needed to understand himself and his ill-fated choices, particularly in women.

His parents divorced when he was eleven years old, after the father's affair was discovered. After that, Andrew rarely saw his alcoholic, workaholic father even though the two had always lived in the same city. Andrew's grandfather, also an alcoholic, treated his own son that way. So the cycle of paternal neglect became a prominent part of Andrew's legacy that he desperately wished to stop before he became a father.

Struggling in a vacuum to figure out how to be a man, Andrew developed a hypermasculinity that had him challenging authority at every turn and relating to women by womanizing. Predictably, his relationship with his mother vacillated from strained to blatantly hostile as he dueled with her over the position of head of the household.

Admitting emotional needs is precarious for men in general because of their socialization. But for Andrew it was extremely risky, because of the myriad ways he had learned to fend off the threat of constant reinjury from his father's neglect.

The following is an excerpt of a session we had in which he began to acknowledge the ache he felt from his father hunger because of their strained and infrequent contact since the divorce.

> **Andrew:** I want to go talk to my father. This week! I think I could tell him now how I've missed him, and how I need him in my life, and how he has to be more than he's been for me to

respect him. *(With profuse tears)* I think we just need to cry in each other's arms and to tell each other we love each other.

Beth: What are your tears for?

Andrew: I need to cry in front of him. It's something I haven't done since I was a child. See, I like him so much! And I really, really, really want to be with him. I just feel like walking into his house and sitting down with him and sobbing.

Beth: What would you be sobbing about?

Andrew: I would be sobbing because I would be pleading and begging him . . .

Beth: To what?

Andrew: To be my father. I miss him, and it's been too long! God! I feel like a kid! *(Winces in pain as tears stream down his face)*

Beth: In many ways, you are. Emotionally. So what are you going to do?

Andrew: I'm going to go see him. Tomorrow. And I'm going to have a heart-to heart talk. But I'll certainly be making myself vulnerable!

When Andrew acknowledged the chronic ache he had always felt from his father's abdication and from his need for him, he could begin to take steps to do something about it. As he crafted a plan to bridge the gap between the two men, he also began to take responsibility both for his needs and for his part in perpetuating the ongoing impasse. Of course, when Andrew was a child, the gulf between father and son was caused by his father's neglect. However, as an adult, Andrew could have exercised different options. Instead he, too, perpetuated the distance. However, once he understood the multiple prices he paid for this, he then could do something about the alienation with his father.

Too often, children are both weapon and prize in divorce wars. And too many are rendered emotionally or actually fatherless in the wake of messy litigation. Yet, researchers have found that the relationship between children and their divorced father is a strong indicator of how well they are able to adjust to divorce, with the quality of the relationship being even more important than frequency of contact.[2] Yet, one study reported that 52 percent of all adolescents age twelve to sixteen who were living with separated, divorced or remarried mothers had not seen their father at all in more than a year, and only 16 percent had seen their father as often as once a week.[3] So, if parents decide that divorce is inevitable, it is incumbent upon them to shield their children from the tragic situation of being wounded either in their marital skirmishes or by a father who abdicates.

Single Mothering

Currently, one out of every three births is to an unmarried mother. In the inner cities of America, 90 percent of children live in households headed by single women. This means that out-of-wedlock births have skyrocketed 600 percent in just three decades, from 5 percent of all births in 1960 to 30 percent in 1991.[4] With the increasing societal acceptance of this trend, of which the sitcom character Murphy Brown is emblematic, there is little reason to believe that this trend will not continue and even increase. Sociologist David Popenoe further predicts that, if the current trend continues, 40 percent of all births (and 80 percent of all minority births) will take place out of wedlock by the turn of the century.[5] Unlike Europe, where out-of-wedlock births occur primarily with cohabiting couples, American children increasingly have little or no relationship with their father. Many children, when asked who their father is, are forced to reply, "I don't have one." Clearly, we live in an era of the shrinking father, where both the mothers who do not make legitimate attempts to help their children maintain contact with their father and fathers who vanish are subjecting their children to suffering father hunger.

When looked at strictly from the woman's point of view, it is easy to comprehend the multiple arguments women use to make and to fortify their decision to become single mothers. As Mary Ann Glendon said, the "rights talk" usually trumps most other considerations when making this decision.[6] The reasoning is that women have a right to choose what happens to their bodies. Women who are self-sufficient should not need, wait for or depend on a man to accomplish life goals. They should be independent and, therefore, do not have to marry. Women should not be expected to give up actualizing the core value of having children just because they cannot find an appropriate man to marry and father their children. Looked at solely from the woman's perspective, all of these arguments are valid. Acting on this reasoning may even indicate a degree of independence and mental health on her part. Likewise, strictly from a man's point of view, it is easy to see how he might conclude that if a woman wants to have sex or have a child, it's her business. And if it's not his choice, why should he feel responsible? Strictly from his point of view, there is logic in these statements.

But what happens to kids who grow up with only one of their biological parents (usually the mother)? The outcomes for many of these children are very different from what most parents who participate ever anticipate.

[Fatherless] children are disadvantaged across a broad array of
outcomes. They are twice as likely to drop out of high school,
2.5 times as likely to become teen-aged mothers and 1.4 times
as likely to be idle—out of school and out of work—as children who grow up with both parents. . . . Loss of economic
resources accounts for about 50 percent of the disadvantages
associated with single parenthood. Too little parental supervision and involvement and greater residential mobility
account for most of the rest.[7]

Sociologist Blankenhorn is more blunt than Popenoe is in
the above quote. "We are generating male violence much faster
than we can incarcerate it. Prisons cannot replace fathers."[8]

Children's personalities and chances in life are formed both
by who cares about and for them, and by how consistent that
care is. The missing ingredient in the single-parent home is
the second adult who can provide parental supervision and
involvement. Intuitively it would seem that others, such as
stepfathers, could make up for this loss. However, the data on
child outcomes shows that children in stepfamilies fare no better than the children of mothers who never marry and that
children are better off with a dead father than a surrogate one.[9]
Further, with the numbers of children living with a divorced
parent or a never-married parent, there is substantial evidence
that having an unmarried father is worse for children than a
divorced father.[10] This is probably due to the fact that, unlike in
Europe, where such births are typically to cohabiting couples,
most nonmarital births in America are to unattached women.
In this way, then, the father's role has been stripped down to
mere conception of the child. And with the advent of artificial
insemination, sometimes fathers are not even present for that.

Blankenhorn refers to these men as "Sperm Fathers," the nameless, faceless embodiment of the misconception that children don't need fathers.[11] They complete their fatherhood by selling their sperm in a test tube for forty dollars. Each year, more and more children in the United States are conceived in these situations.

Single motherhood may seem the ideal solution for women who want to create manless families and for men willing or eager to embrace sex and procreation without fatherhood. But in short, these men too often represent the tiniest fragment of fatherhood imaginable and are living evidence of our society's growing belief that fathers are irrelevant or superfluous.

Ami: "What Have I Done to My Children?"

She was a single mother in her early twenties with two children, ages seven and four. Ami had previously thought her children's contact with their father was optional and even unnecessary, until she took my family studies course. Reflecting the socialized messages she received from our culture, she thought she was Superwoman who could single-handedly provide for all of her children's wants and needs to grow up healthily. Here, in a class assignment, she eloquently described her dawning realization of how her and their father's choices have impacted their children as well as what she observes about them. Although she notes that the children know their father, she really thinks of them as not having one.

> After our class discussion on pregnancy and childbirth, I became very confused. The specific topic which confused me, was how important it is for a child to have two parents involved in their life. My children, ages seven and four, only

have one *involved* parent. I have always wondered what impact this will have on my children. Of course, I have always rationalized the effects of this.

My kids do know their father and have very occasional contact with him. He does, usually, attend very important functions, like birthdays or sporting events. The day-to-day activities, which many times produce important events, are left unnoticed. He usually never even hears about these types of events. I have always just figured that since he doesn't want to be involved, why should I bother to force him? When I start feeling bad, I tell myself that it is not that big of a deal and that I can make up for what their father is not giving.

After this discussion, I am wondering if this will have long-term negative results on my kids. I am also looking at past events, and I am trying to determine if their not having a father has played a role in these events. For example, my son is having difficulties in school. He is in a special education classroom, and his teachers are now sure it is A.D.D. Now I am looking back, and I am wondering if his father, or lack of one, has played a role in this.

Clearly, it is not the sole responsibility of Ami, an already overburdened single mother, to ensure the participation of an *apparently* disinterested father. However, I wonder about whether this father's minimal participation in his children's lives is a function of his acceptance of our culture's trend toward the shrinking father. I also speculate about the messages Ami may be sending to everyone that the children belong to her. Since she had both children by the same father, she obviously knew what an uninvolved father he would be the second time, if not the first. So apparently she, too, accepted the belief currently in vogue that fathers are irrelevant as her children's dad goes blithely on his way.

The ones who pay for their parents' conclusions and the choices that arise from them are children who are consigned to a life without father either in the home or involved in their lives in any meaningful way. This lack of a relationship with their father leaves them with a gnawing void. Most cope either by low-grade depression or by erecting monumental defenses so they can seem unaffected.

How might these fathers respond if mothers and educators routinely invited their participation, rather than accepting at face value the fathers' apparent disinterest? Clearly, these modest measures would not always kindle the interest of the uninvolved parent. However, they may begin to reverse the growing message that fathers are irrelevant in children's lives and help fathers learn even minimal ways to participate. For those children whose fathers might become involved, these rudimentary steps are worth attempting. All children and our culture as a whole need us to seek the great changes that potentially may come from these small interventions. As Senator Daniel Patrick Moynihan once observed, a society of unattached males "asks for and gets chaos."[12]

Above all, it is hoped that women who contemplate single mothering will seriously consider the multiple ramifications of exercising that prerogative. Indeed, it is a matter of urgent importance that they grasp what their children, especially their sons, will be up against if they never know their father. Before they make this irreversible decision, they also need to reckon with what this could mean for them as solo parents of children who will know the distress of the nagging, ongoing grief of father hunger.

Adoption

The face of contemporary adoption has changed dramatically. Whereas in the past, the majority of those adopted were infants adopted by couples, today there are three other situations where children are adopted. First, babies are not the only children being put up for adoption; minors of any age from first marriages that end in divorce are often relinquished by birth fathers to stepfathers. Second, more and more single mothers are seeking adoption. And third, more and more lesbian and gay couples are adopting. *There is no doubt that being adopted into a family is clearly preferable to living in an institution or a string of foster homes.* Still, there are some special considerations that parents of adopted children need to keep in mind.

When parents of young children divorce, it is increasingly common that first fathers relinquish their parental role and rights to stepfathers and then drop out of sight, as Melanie's father did. However, while children are the predisposing factor for couples staying in first marriages, in subsequent marriages, conflict centered on them often prompts couples to divorce. The statistics about the success of second marriages with children are dismal, with 65 percent of them ending in divorce.[13] Then these children, already abandoned by one father, often are abandoned again if this marriage does not work out. Presumably, fathers who disappear and those who step up to the line in their place both believe they are acting in their children's best interests. However, it is incumbent upon mothers and stepfathers in these situations to take extra precautions to ensure that this child is not abandoned again through another divorce, or if divorce is inevitable, to together invest in the child's ongoing contact with the stepfather. Otherwise, these children can be expected to learn to trust no one because their prototype for relationships, their parents, cannot be counted on to stay.

The second and third situations are similar, from a child's point of view. We have already discussed what children of single mothers experience when they do not know their fathers. It is similar for adoptees of gay and lesbian couples. They, too, end up with little or no information about either birth parent. But they have the additional knowledge gap of no personal experience with people of one or the other sex. These children can be expected to have significant issues with father hunger with which they—and their parents—will have to cope. This is not reason enough not to adopt. However, parents need to go into such a situation with their eyes open.

Regardless of whether the adoption takes place in infancy or later in a child's life after the birth father's abdication, all adoptions share two significant common elements. Adopted children know only shadows where fathers are supposed to be. This leaves them with skewed pictures of fathers and of men, and with gaping holes in their identities and in their souls, resulting in father hunger that can mount to craving. Like families of POWs and MIAs, they experience an ambiguous loss. If the birth father has totally disappeared, they never know whether their father will be found or not, even if they search. It is always harder to make peace with an ambiguous loss than a definitive one because there is no finite end point from which one can move on. Betty Jean Lifton, an adoptee herself, wrote, "We must consider that there is nowhere to go from nowhere."[14] Even those who search for and eventually locate their birth father experience the same kind of nagging, ongoing loss that infertile couples know because it is a relationship that never was. Again quoting Lifton, "The adoptee is forced to lead a double existence: the surface one which he shares with his adoptive family, and the secret one which is like a lost Atlantis sunken in his entrails." [15]

Adoptive parents may tell their children over and over that they were chosen, but the reality is that most will have great difficulty believing that they matter. Many feel stolen or dumped. No matter how often adopted children are told that their new parents are now their "real" parents, they can never completely ignore their birth parents and the fact that they gave them up. Fathers particularly remain an ambiguous loss for many adoptees because many never search for them, perhaps because of our culture's messages that fathers are optional.

Alicia: "I Only Knew His Last Name"

Here is a case of a forty-two-year-old mother of three teenage sons and one preschooler. Divorced from her older son's father, Alicia began dating a man with a chronic fear of commitment. Although they also had a son, after eight years, Alicia was tired of Ray's postponing their on-again, then off-again wedding plans. What was worse, just as they would become comfortable in their relationship, she would discover that Ray had again been with another woman. What prompted their request for couples therapy was that this time Alicia was fed up and planned to end the relationship because Ray had fathered another woman's child. Her resolve appeared firm, despite the fact that they shared a child and Ray successfully had assumed the role of dad for her teenage sons. Although it agonized her to contemplate life without him, she felt she had been humiliated one too many times. Her resolve this time finally caught Ray's attention, and he called for an emergency intake appointment, which they both attended with high hopes.

When they began treatment, they both literally acted out their anxious/ambivalent attachment styles; their difficulty with trusting and being trustworthy; and their arrested development around appropriate levels of separation and individuation. Just when they would get close, one or the other would orchestrate a crisis so that they could justify distancing from each other again. And yet, despite both of their protestations to the contrary, they were stuck together like Siamese twins, unable to individuate enough from each other to take responsibility for their own feelings, needs and actions. The pattern of their swings was so extreme that I worried aloud that they might be a couple who couldn't stand to be together but couldn't stand to be apart. If this were the case, there would have been no way I—or anyone—could help them out of their purgatory.

Because each was so fearful of intimacy for legitimate reasons, joint sessions deteriorated easily into a debate, a shouting match or a trial. This, of course, entrenched them in their pattern and fueled their hopelessness even more. So, after the third huge crisis they unconsciously had orchestrated to avoid genuinely facing either themselves or each other, I decided to try a course of individual therapy for each. I even refused to do any more joint sessions—even if the couple generated another brouhaha—until both began to confront their feelings.

I began the individual sessions by drawing each of their family trees to collect information to help them understand and modify the contribution each was making to their misery. From Alicia I learned that her first husband had committed

suicide after threatening to do so throughout their entire marriage. I also learned that a family had adopted her in infancy
from a woman who was her adoptive mother's best friend.
This made the woman—whom she had known all her life as
her adoptive mother's friend—her birth mother. However,
even though she had been given this information as an eight-
year-old, no one had helped her talk about or understand it.
So it went underground until she told me. At that, it took her
several sessions to exhume the information she had buried and
then to begin dealing with it. Here we see her grapple with the
poverty of information she had about her birth father and how
this void affected her.

Beth: What do you think we should work with today?
Alicia: I don't know. I've thought about your comment that I
don't trust anyone. And I thought about it, and I thought about
it, and I guess you're right.
Beth: So I'll bet that would have a lot to do with how you
work with and feel about Ray.
Alicia: It sure does! It has to go back to the fact that I never
knew my birth father.

Beth: What do you know about him?
Alicia: Very little! I know his last name. And I only know that.
You look as confused as I am!
Beth: I am! And if *I'm* confused, I can imagine how you feel!
Alicia: Yes! It's like you said one day, and I've thought about
it. All those issues I thought I'd put away and moved on, I
guess I haven't.
Beth: How do you think all this confusion has affected you,
just the confusion itself?

Alicia: I think, in my relationships with men . . . I worry that the people in my life are going to leave me. *(With profuse tears)* I guess, as I grew up . . . I knew I was different, but I didn't know *how*. And I learned about all of this when my brother was sick with leukemia, and then he passed away. So once again, somebody I loved left.

Beth: How did you find out that you were adopted?

Alicia: My brother and I were sitting on the porch one day. I was eight, and he was sixteen. He said, "You are my sister, but you are my adopted sister." And I'll tell you, time stood still! And I thought he was going to ask me to go to the store! I grew up thinking I was different. But when he said that, things fell into place. I always had to explain why I was different, so when he finally told me, things fell into place.

Beth: Where does trust fit into all of this?

Alicia: Gee, that's interesting. I guess there's a part of me that thinks if I don't give my trust, I won't get hurt so easily. But I end up getting hurt anyway. Am I with you?

Beth: You sure are! And for reasons I don't exactly understand, I'm thinking about your birth father right now. I wonder what's the connection here.

Alicia: I think my birth father is the reason I don't trust men. I feel like he just wiped his hands clean and said, "I did all I could." He just never gave it another thought. In fairness to him, maybe nobody told him, but I just thought I didn't matter!

Beth: Wowie!

Alicia: But I don't *know* that he didn't try. I was just too consumed by my own pain to even think about him.

Beth: What do you think your pain has been about?

Alicia: Growing up, I thought he didn't care. You know, everything I'm saying today, I've said to myself, but I've never said it out loud.

Beth: Why not?

Alicia: Because I've thought, *Who would I say it to?* I did tell Ray one night, and he fell asleep, so I never brought it up again. Of course, it's not his fault because he was dog-tired. No fault of his.

Beth: Ouch! So you set yourself up. What I mean is, when the only male in your life that was trustworthy left, although he didn't ask to die, men leaving is normal for you. And when kids have that experience, they become active in bringing it about—unconsciously, but actively.

Alicia: I realize that now, although I didn't realize until you just pointed it out that I do that! And it's still scary. It's real scary! No one likes to air out their dirty laundry. And sometimes we have dirty laundry, and we don't even know it!

Here Alicia begins to grasp key elements that have formed her psychological makeup and contribute to the couple's disastrous relationship dynamic. It is interesting that merely pondering the question of trust took her directly to her birth father. She began to piece together some of the effects of her having just a scintilla of information about her birth father where a relationship with him, or at least knowledge of him, should be. In its place is a profound sense of confusion, identity diffusion, abandonment and personal rejection. As a result, she learned to expect to be abandoned. And to be in control of something, she repetitively chose men who would bring about her abandonment.

Gradually, she began to connect the dots about how Ray's terror of commitment fit the script formed in her infancy and reinforced by her beloved brother's untimely death. The promise inherent in her understanding is not to blame herself or anyone, for that matter. Rather, it is to empower herself. When she knew her part in the dance, she could change her steps. And if she had had Ray's cooperation, together they might have choreographed a new ballet. However, Ray chose to keep running, and eventually she gained the strength and the insight to take some qualitatively different actions. Eventually, she left the relationship, a sadder but wiser woman.

Addiction

Children whose parents were addicted must often cope with multiple sources of father hunger. One comes from the wars waged on them by the addiction, some from the various forms of abuse and neglect that too often accompany substance abuse, and still more comes from the distraction of the sober parent who must cope with the addicted spouse. One workshop participant spent much of his adolescence sitting across the street from his father's favorite tavern, hoping to catch a glimpse of his drunken father whom his mother had divorced because of his addiction. Seeing his father come staggering out was the only remnant of fathering he could scrape together. Much like children of abusive fathers, children of addicted fathers frequently feel abandoned by both parents because neither is psychologically safe. The result is children who feel invisible, not truly seen by either parent.

Further, the loosening of inhibitions that accompanies being high leaves the conditions ripe for physical, sexual and emotional abuse. Thus, a situation develops where chaos is natural and where normal is boring. But even when the father

is a "nice drunk," it is still difficult for children to feel safe.
This consigns these children to lives where turmoil becomes
preferable and where anxiety, never feeling good enough and
quiet despair are a way of life.

Brenda: Neither Seen nor Heard

As a thirty-five-year-old mother of two, Brenda stumbled
onto some frightening but dim childhood memories when her
marriage of twelve years fell apart. Because it literally took
most of those twelve years for her to realize that her husband
was physically, sexually and emotionally abusive to her, she
sought therapy to understand how she got into such a marriage
in the first place and, more importantly, why she stayed. Since
the roots of this irrational behavior generally are in the family
of origin, we probed her childhood for answers to her questions. Not surprisingly, we discovered her father's multiple
unresolved losses that he anesthetized with booze. Still
haunted as an adult, the self-absorption and self-medication of
Brenda's father caused her, in turn, to lose his presence in any
meaningful sense.

The following excerpt takes place as Brenda's denial began
to thaw enough for her to realize the emotional neglect she
suffered from both parents because of her father's drinking.
Even so, she still did touch-and-go landings to avoid the subject.

Beth: Has your father ever made eye contact with you?
Brenda: It's when he's been angry or really pushing a point.
Or when he's drunk. It's usually late in the evening, about
9:30, so he's really drunk.
Brenda: One day last week, I woke up having a dream of
myself when I was three or four. It had to do with nobody in

my house seeing me. My siblings did, but my parents didn't. It was like I didn't matter.

Beth: What sense do you think you made out of no one seeing you?

Brenda: I got the message that what I wanted didn't matter. And yet, I had some sexual power that I could use.

Beth: What do you think you told yourself about that?

Brenda: I don't recall telling myself anything.

Beth: I'll bet you told yourself something.

Brenda: I think I told myself I was bad. I can tell you honestly that the first time I felt I had a reason to live was when I had my first child. And I was twenty-eight! *(With tears rimming her eyes)* And that's pretty sad! She was the first person who unconditionally loved me. My parents didn't even see me. My father told me once that he loved me, and at that point I was in my thirties.

Beth: What are the feelings that go with saying that?

Brenda: It's just a pit. A stainless steel pit.

Beth: And it's cold and hard.

Brenda: And it doesn't dent easily. I don't know. I don't know how to get through all of this. I think about my father dying, and I think, "Good! Then my mom won't have to live with him anymore."

Beth: So you're really angry.

Brenda: It doesn't feel like anger. But I am feeling chest pain.

Beth: Touché! *(Commenting on her defensive maneuver of converting her emotions to physical pain)* You really are agile!

Brenda: *(With tears in her eyes)* No, I'm not. I'm stuck.

Brenda was invisible despite being an honors student, a cheerleader and a talented musician. And because either being

invisible or being abused were all she had known, she had
married a man who continued this treatment of her. Only, not
surprisingly, his abusive behavior was even more extreme.
However, until she understood this and resolved it, it would be
virtually impossible for her to do anything else. But even
knowing this, it was a long road to being seen, which began
with seeing and knowing herself.

Abuse

In families where parents are not grown up, children are
robbed of their childhood. Although adults demonstrate that they
are emotional and intellectual children in many ways, the potentially most scarring and deadly effects on their children involves
abuse. Here, adults' inability to empathize and to think abstractly
about themselves and their behavior is most apparent.

Although all abusive behavior involves a problem with
impulse control, I am not referring to the potential anyone has
to momentarily lose control with a child and impulsively act in
ways that immediately are regretted. While certainly jarring for
everyone, it probably is not a loss for the children whose parents apologize and do not abuse again. From this, children learn
that everyone is human and that parents can be trusted to have
concern for the children's welfare. By contrast, habitually abusive fathers, even if there is guilt and remorse after the abusive
act, remain unreliable and untrustworthy to the child. Because
children never know when the next storm will brew or what it
will be about, they usually cope by keeping a physical and emotional distance from the perpetrating parent. Sadly, this protective distance creates a loss of the abusive parent. And because
they often observe that the nonperpetrating parent is ineffectual

in stopping the abuse or, worse yet, appears to give tacit approval, they also experience the other parent as emotionally unsafe. So abused children often are emotional orphans.

However, when children become adults, they no longer are dependent on their parents' beneficence or limited by their lack of psychological resources. When they are big, strong and intellectually capable of defending themselves, they can talk with the abuser about what happened. Like nothing else, it helps salve wounds and correct developmental arrests. Although there generally is colossal fear about facing the titanic abuser, for many it is an essential part of healing not only the abused but also the abusive family dynamics. Forgiving the abusive father and his feeling forgiven truly provide the balm of a corrective emotional experience. Even if the father denies the abuse, just speaking your truth and acknowledging your feelings goes a long way toward stopping the ripple effects that have continued since childhood. But nothing resolves abused children's father loss more than talking with them about the hurt, having it acknowledged, hearing an apology and granting forgiveness. Such a conversation can end the emotional ripple effects the abuse has perpetuated, even though the abuse in reality stopped years ago.

Matt: The Terrified Gentle Giant

Lisa and Matt came to therapy when he could not extricate himself from a highly verbally abusive wife. I worked many months to intervene in the couple's explosive interactions to teach them more healthy alternatives, but I had little success. Their fights were increasing, rather than the opposite, and escalating to Lisa's hitting and biting Matt. So when Lisa requested separate sessions for a time to work on their separate issues, I readily complied.

As I searched for contributors to his terror of Lisa, Matt quietly confessed with a great deal of embarrassment that he was still afraid of his father, even though he felt protective of him, which was exactly how he felt toward Lisa. Looking at Matt, it would be difficult to imagine how he could be afraid of anyone. He weighed 365 pounds, stood six feet, six inches tall, and had been a wrestler and football player all through high school and college. His father was his high school coach, so Matt saw the man as a combination of Dad, mentor, coach, giant and tormentor. Because he was stuck still viewing his father from a child's vantage point and because his love for the man was fierce, it took me six months to convince Matt to talk directly with his father about his childhood. But finally, he relented, and the parents flew in from the East Coast to meet with us.

Seeing the father was a jarring experience for me. I expected the man to be even bigger than his son, to match the mental picture Matt had painted of him. Instead, he was a head shorter and a hundred pounds lighter than his son. Still, Matt quaked in his presence, regressing to that emotionally stuck eight-year-old—Matt's age when the abuse began. Even with size, maturity and me on his side, as he began preparing for these sessions, he reexperienced the same fears he had when he was eight. Part of the preparation was helping him plan how to manage his fears and take care of himself even in the face of this man who indeed was larger than life to Matt. This itself was an integral part of Matt's corrective emotional experience.

Although the father had only occasionally exploded into abusiveness, the terror that these episodes begot left the boy frozen at a great self-protective distance from his father. This had been a poignant loss for both men. The following excerpt is a slice of the first hour in a four-hour family-of-origin session.

Matt: *(With tears streaming down his face)* I want your help getting back to that eight-year-old kid and letting him know there wasn't anything he did to deserve being hit or yelled at.

Dad: *(Defensive at first)* I don't think what I did was abuse. But it sounds like you think it was. It wasn't what you did; it was the way I reacted to it. And that's my problem. It was instantaneous rage. You've got to understand what I'm saying. There is no one in the world I'm prouder of! *(In tears, glowering at the therapist)* I wasn't going to do this!

Beth: What's it like seeing your daddy's tears?

Matt: It's really nice, *(Crying harder)* It makes me know you cared. But I want to know that I didn't deserve what happened.

Dad: I don't think there's *any* question [of that]! It wasn't you, it was me. My stepdad beat me with everything he could. He just graduated. When razor straps didn't make me cry any more, he graduated to a baseball bat. Planning to kill him until I was sixteen was part of what I did to you. I'm not making an excuse, please understand. I'm just trying to give you an explanation. You've got to understand, that was *my* mentality. It had nothing to do with you.

Matt: *(Referring to our discussions of transgenerational patterns)* I realize that I'm a product not only of what you went through, but what they went though. But I thought I was gonna die!

Dad: I can understand how you'd take it that way. Especially when I think of it from the standpoint of an eight-year-old.

Matt: I was so afraid of you I would do anything. I wanted to be tough.

Dad: In these past few years, I've sensed there was a wall between us. I would have done anything in the world to keep from hurting you! What you never understood is that I'd have given up my life in two seconds for you. *(Sobbing)* What you've got to understand is that you're the pride of my life! *(Dad initiates a hug)* I love my family more than life itself!
Matt: I know, I know. But it helps to hear. I love you so much! I'm so glad you're still here to do this with!
Dad: They say you can't go back. But when you do this, you do.
Matt: *(As if having just made a remarkable discovery)* I know you love me!
Dad: I hope you do!

As this excerpt ends, the two men sob, in the center of the room, locked in a hug that lasted four delicious minutes. In these precious moments, both men began healing. Matt, with his father's help, could begin to heal the chronic ache from the loss of his father, born of the toxic combination of abuse and distancing to protect himself from the father's unpredictability and rage.

Traditional Fathering

Losses from traditional fathers are perhaps the most subtle and difficult for clinicians to diagnose and for clients to acknowledge. These are the everyday losses that people have difficulty naming because of their daily contact with their emotionally unavailable father. Nowhere is the contradiction between "real man" and "good father" more evident than with them.

What is a traditional father? Because the role of nurturer customarily has been delegated to mothers, traditional fathers have been socialized to take the roles of good provider and firm disciplinarian. However, the evidence suggests that fathers who rigidly remain in a cold, detached role with their children have a negative impact on them. Doing so impedes the psychological development of fathers as well because this leaves fathers emotionally distant from their children when at home, and physically absent because of their rigid adherence to their role prescription.

Ironically, even with men's increasing awareness that they and their presence are important in the lives of their children, it may be that children of the 1990s will experience father hunger not unlike their fathers' own from their 1950s traditional fathers. This is because, since the 1960s, despite the advent of technological advances, the number of hours that people work has increased. Our current ethic of consumerism has elevated keeping up with the Joneses to the status of a new religion. Yet, few parents realize that the choice usually is between giving their children time or money, and that generally they cannot give both. Still fewer appear to realize that it is more important to most children for parents to give of themselves and of their time. So, with the expectations placed on families by our culture's materialistic demands, fathers often are absent to "feed" their families not food but designer jeans, lessons, braces and private schools.

Jerry: "Where Were You When I Needed You?"

It took four years of cajoling to convince Jerry, a highly successful man in his early fifties, that he needed to confess to his father the ache he had felt for him since childhood because of his need for his unavailable traditional father. The following excerpt is the climax of approximately two and a half years of struggling. First, the son had to be encouraged and helped to say what truly was on his mind. Then it seemed to take the father an eternity to even grasp the meaning of the questions his son was asking. And finally, the father needed to be prompted to give the response his son needed now.

Beth: *(To Jerry)* Do you know what I think part of this *(refer-ring to his fist that he has clenched during most of the session)* has been? I think it's anger.

Jerry: Yeah, probably.

Beth: And I think a lot of it's about your dad, at your dad.

Jerry: Yeah. I mean, it's what I've been trying to let go of.

Beth: Yeah, but you've not told him directly, "Dad, I've been angry."

Jerry: No. I suppose that's true. I guess that's true. *(To his father)* I talked a little bit yesterday about the feelings I remember. And I think they're the ones that I hold old anger about, and they're the reason I hold you apart or push you away. And it's anger at your not being there.

Beth: Tell him about that.

Jerry: You just weren't there. All the important stuff that you had to do, and those people at work were more important than me.

Beth: How did that make you feel?

Jerry: All alone! All alone, even with the family around and in the house, with stuff to do, all alone, because those people at work were more important than me. And that's where the anger comes from.

Beth: Because it hurts.

Jerry: Yeah, it hurts! And right around behind that anger is fear that just goes along and makes it even worse. It's fear for your reaction if I tell you how I feel.

Dad: Well, I feel badly about this.

Mom: Say, "I love you, Jerry."

Dad: I do love you, Jerry! You know that!

Jerry: *(Almost inaudibly)* I don't know if I know that.

Dad: Huh?

Jerry: *(Crying softly)* I don't know if I know that!

Dad: Well, I'll tell you. And I'll show you.

Beth: Tell him what your tears are, Jerry.

Jerry: That's the first real time I've heard "I will!" instead of saying, "We'll work on it." You said, "I will," and I believe you.

Dad: Yes, I will!

Jerry: *(Crying harder)* But don't let me down. Don't let me down!

Beth: Tell him about it, Jerry.

Jerry: Just don't . . . you just can't stop. You know I've got a process started, and I got this far, and we got this far, and I want you to know that I just can't have you back away. *(Sobbing)* Don't leave! Don't disappear!

Dad: *(Putting his arms around Jerry)* You know I won't.

Jerry: No, I don't know that you won't! And that's what I need. I don't know that you won't.

Dad: Well, I'll show you!

Jerry: That's what I have to have! I don't know that you won't. We've gone this far, and I've gotta trust that you'll be there. That's what I need. I just need you to be there. The words are fine now. But when we walk out of this room, and when we're at the table or on the phone, I just need you to be there.

Dad: It's the follow-through that counts.

Beth: 'Cause it's so scary to let yourself count on his being there, and risk disappointment again.

Jerry: Yeah, 'cause I'll fold. That's how important it is, Dad.

Beth: That's how important you are, Dad.

Jerry: That's how important it is that you're there.

Dad: I'll be there!

The weekend following our meetings was the parents' anniversary celebration, which the family celebrated with a weekend at a country inn in a neighboring town. Over dinner the first night, Jerry and his wife had an argument, and she sped away from the restaurant, leaving Jerry to walk the short distance back to the inn. About a block from the hotel, Jerry's dad appeared out of the darkness (despite his difficulty walking after a recent stroke), asking if there was anything he could do. Jerry replied, "Just walk with me." Words were not necessary. So the two men walked in a companionable silence that felt deeply comforting to Jerry, now that the men had a blueprint for how to be different with each other. Just being together can be the height of contentment and intimacy, if people's silence is not because of fear or ambivalence.

Jerry called me about a year later to say that his father had finally died of another stroke. And it was a very different experience from the one Jerry had always expected before our sessions. Instead of standing over the casket railing and then dancing on the grave, he stood in both places quietly crying. Now he felt sad but blessed. He finally felt privileged to have a father he could and would miss.

Three Precautions

First, in the excerpts that involved actual conversations with fathers, you no doubt noticed that initially there was a struggle getting them to hear and to address their children's feelings and needs. Expecting yourselves to broach this painful and delicate subject on your own with your father and to resolve everyone's feelings may be hoping for too much. If you truly have no other option, proceed with caution. If outside help is available, grab it so you do not have to face this painful and anxiety-provoking situation alone. The help of a skilled and sensitive therapist will markedly decrease the chances of a hand grenade blowing up in everyone's face.

Second, it is most conducive to healing wounds from the past to *talk with*—not *confront*—your parent(s). While it is important that you have their reality validated and no longer denied, you most likely will hear that admission if both client and counselor are careful not to engage the parents' defenses. In short, confront the abuse, not the abuser. Face the truth of your situation with empathy and understanding for how your father handled you and his life. And even if he does not acknowledge that his behavior was harmful, it usually may be enough to tell him this is how you saw it and felt.

Third, if such a conversation is to be facilitated by a professional, make certain that this person understands that the first goal is to help you maintain or build a connection to your lost father rather than to burn bridges. Too much of what is passed off as therapeutic is really professionally induced and sanctioned parental alienation. All parents, no matter how heinous their actions, need to feel concern and even empathy from the therapist in order to open up and acknowledge the damage done by their behavior, no matter how unwittingly.

Social Implications

Children telegraph their pain through their conduct, because they have no abstract concepts and, therefore, few words for their internal experience. In this era of the epidemic rise of gangs, juvenile delinquency, teen pregnancy, school underachievement and the pestilence left in their wake, we as a society can ill afford to leave any stone unturned in searching for solutions. To the extent that absent fathers and denying mothers are contributing, however unwittingly, to the growing war in our schools and our cities, neither children nor our culture as a whole can afford to see their fathers as luxuries or disposable commodities. And yet, as Mary Pipher, quoting Joshua Meyrowitz, wrote in her book *The Shelter of Each Other,* "We are becoming a nation of neither children nor adults. Rather we all exist in some age zone between childhood and adulthood. We're a nation of adolescents—preoccupied with ourselves, sexualized, moody and impulsive, seeking freedom without responsibility."[16] It is a matter of grave importance that we wake up to the multiple and severe social and emotional prices paid by children, their families, and ultimately by our society for the removal of fathers from families and from the lives of children.

ACTION EXERCISE

Do You Experience Father Hunger?

This exercise is designed to help you trace your father's imprint on your life. Ultimately, it will help you discern whether or not you experience father hunger, in case this is not already apparent to you.

Reflect on the following questions.

- Who do you think of as your "real father"?
- If not your birth father, why not?
- How have you explained that to yourself over the years?

- Did anyone else attempt to help you understand his place in your life?
- If so, who did, and how was it explained?
- If your father was absent, were you allowed and even encouraged to ask questions about this?
- How old were you when you last saw your birth father?
- Reconstruct the events and circumstances of that last visit.
- When was the last time you had fun with your father?
- Did you blame yourself for your father's absence?

After you complete this exercise, mentally step back and make some observations about your responses. How did your experiences with your father script your feelings and behavior with men? How does your relationship with your father influence what you want from and how you behave in relationships?

Increasingly the distinction between *haves* and *have-nots* will not be economic; it will be between those who have meaningful contact with their father and those who don't.[17] Yet, unlike mothers, fathers are less born than made. Do all children need and deserve a relationship with their father? "Our [society's] current answer hovers between 'no' and 'not necessarily.'"[18] With the messages rampant in our culture about fatherhood being voluntary, we can expect an increase in the incidence of father hunger. This is despite many of the current generation of infants who are being reared by two involved parents. Enough fathers are opting to make this the core domestic challenge facing our country at the close of this century and this millennium. More than any other factor, fatherlessness is contributing to the decline of children's well-being in this country. Because of this, we are creating a society riddled by the twin nightmare of too many little boys with guns and too many little girls with babies.[19]

Saying a Good Good-Bye

There can be happy endings to the painful condition of father loss. Oren, from whom we heard at the beginning of this chapter, offers us one such example. It is worthy of note that when Oren and I began to explore the impact of the relationships he had with both of his fathers, he felt very confident about being able to contact his birth father on his own. So he and his new wife flew halfway across the country to see him for the first time in twenty-five years. And it was a joyous reunion, which became the first of many.

However, facing his stepfather was much more difficult. So he and his wife requested my help for a session that ended thirty years of alienation. And were they ever fortunate! Less than three years after our session, the stepfather died from a rare form of cancer. At the funeral, Oren offered the following eulogy, which he delivered facing the man he now called Dad, who was lying in an open casket.

Dad,

Eulogies are new to me, but I wanted to say publicly to all of the people present the things that I have had a chance to say to you privately. Perhaps I'm a good choice for a eulogy because our relationship has gone through some very rough periods lasting many years.

About three years ago after more than thirty years of being

angry, I decided to do something different. But you beat me to it. For the first time ever, you called me and said that you felt you had made some mistakes as a father. You said that you wanted to send me a videotape of a PBS program you had been watching and then discuss it with me by phone. Instead I suggested you join me in counseling, and in less than five seconds you said yes, knowing that I needed to clear the air and it would not be easy for either of us.

Less than one month later, you spent a week with us, including several hours in counseling, where we put all of the cards on the table. You told me about the family you grew up in, and at sixty-seven years old, you cried when you talked about mistakes you made as a dad when I was a boy and how you wanted it to be better now.

For the past two and a half years, I have been able to set aside the anger about what I didn't have, and acknowledge the gifts that you gave me, and allow myself to see a very different side of you.

Dad, I have heard so many friends and acquaintances in their forties and fifties say that they had waited until it was too late to say the things that they needed to say to their dads. We didn't. Thanks for letting me be so honest with you and for being honest with me. Thanks for taking huge risks in order to bring your oldest son back home. Thanks for being my dad when my other dad went away. Thanks for doing the best you knew how in being my father.

I miss you.

Good-bye, Dad.

—Oren

References

1. David Popenoe, *Life Without Father* (New York: Free Press, 1996), 6.

2. Ibid., 150.

3. Ibid., 31.

4. Ibid., 6.

5. Ibid., 77.

6. Mary Ann Glendon as quoted in David Blankenhorn, *Fatherless America: Confronting Our Most Urgent Social Problem* (New York: Basic Books, 1995), 20.

7. Popenoe, *Life Without Father,* 9.

8. David Blankenhorn, *Fatherless America: Confronting Our Most Urgent Social Problem* (New York: Basic Books, 1995), 20.

9. Popenoe, *Life Without Father,* 9.

10. Ibid., 23.

11. Blankenhorn, *Fatherless America,* 32.

12. Popenoe, *Life Without Father,* 91.

13. William Galston, "Divorce American Style," *Public Interest* 126 (summer 1996): 12-26.

14. Betty Jean Lifton, *Lost and Found: The Adoption Experience* (New York: Harper & Row, 1988), 65.

15. Ibid., 21.

16. Mary Pipher, *The Shelter of Each Other: Rebuilding Our Families* (New York: G.P. Putnam's Sons, 1996), 18.

17. Blankenhorn, *Fatherless America,* 95.

18. Ibid., 222.

19. Popenoe, *Life Without Father,* 63.

PART TWO

Effects of
Father Loss
in Adulthood

5

When Dick and Jane Grow Up: Fathers, Sons and Daughters

Now, we've made the revolutionary discovery that children have two parents. A decade ago, even the kindly Dr. Spock held mothers solely responsible for children.

—Gloria Steinem
Outrageous Acts and Everyday Rebellions

By now, it is clear that children who experience little or no relationship with their father are harmed. Are males and females impacted differently? Are there any similarities in how both sexes are affected?

As significant a force as my father was in my life, he was not perfect. Though he was an active participant in my life until I was nine years old, I still experienced a measure of father hunger, even before he died. This happened in the service of my socialization as a good girl and out of allegiance to my family's expectations not to discuss feelings. As one might expect, this potent combination set me up for emotional disaster.

When I was two and one-half years old, I had an accident when I proudly was being mommy's little helper in the kitchen. I severely burned my entire arm by clumsily submerging it in a pot of boiling soup that Mother was preparing for the family's evening meal. I remember the incident vividly. Mama nearly fainted when she saw how badly I was hurt. She frantically called Daddy, who rushed home from work to go with us to the doctor. I still can smell the pungent ointment my parents were instructed to slather on my arm. It took a long time for it to heal as the skin dropped off my arm in sheets. The only bright spot was that Daddy sought me out every day when he came home from work. He would carry me to his favorite chair in the living room, set me on his lap and ask how much it hurt that day. Because the burn was severe, it took a long time to stop hurting. But I remember not letting Daddy know. Instead, I proudly placed an imaginary mark with my pudgy little finger to show him how much less it supposedly hurt each day.

Already by the age of two and one-half, I had learned my family's code of silence about emotions. Already I had internalized what I had to do to be a good girl: take care of others and submerge my own needs in favor of theirs. Already my pain didn't matter. In my socialized female's quest for closeness, I had internalized that I was to conceal my genuine reactions in order to preserve connections. Ironically, even though Daddy asked, I apparently did not feel as though I could be open. This experience, of course, both foreshadowed and shaped the difficulty I would have with acknowledging my feelings, either to a partner or to myself well into adulthood.

However, because I was a toddler, I was oblivious to these subtleties. I only knew that I loved my daddy unequivocally and would do anything to preserve the attention I got from him. And I thrived on it, realizing only many years later the price I paid for taking it upon myself to ensure it.

Family Rules Are Sometimes More Potent Than Socialization

Some families, for reasons unique to them, cause their children to override their gender socialization. As was discussed in chapter 3, family rules can be potent guides for behavior. Sometimes, the ways families operate train people to respond in ways that are markedly different from the norm for their sex. For example, my family's rule prohibiting the outward expression of emotion took precedence over our culture's general acceptance of females expressing emotions. In other instances, girls may, for their own reasons and based on their own family experiences, develop a persona of toughness and ridicule anything that is typically female. And boys may develop the soft, typically feminine side of their personality instead of the rough, competitive part that usually is associated with maleness. Thus, people's coping styles and the subsequent relationship dysfunction that those patterns create, especially for people with unresolved father loss, can be said to lie at the intersection of cultural and family messages. Ruth Ann provides an example of this phenomenon.

Ruth Ann: "Anything You Can Do I Can Do Better"

Ruth Ann and Duane came to therapy when the power struggles that had riddled their ten-year marriage were becoming so precarious that they seemed to be tottering on the edge of both bankruptcy and divorce. Like Nero, who fiddled while Rome burned, they had been forced to relinquish their dream house to meet the financial obligation that mounted while they argued.

The couple had met while white-water rafting. Both avid mountain climbers, they prided themselves on being tough daredevils who weren't afraid of anything. Because relationships are perhaps the most daring adventure of life, the irony was that they seemed to be extremely frightened of each other. While both could be contenders if there were a World's Biggest Thug contest, Ruth Ann surely would win hands down. I concluded that they were emotional terrorists whose intimacy fears had run amok. So I set about trying to tease out why.

Ruth Ann was the oldest of five daughters. Her mother, who she now truly understands because she has five children of her own, was overwhelmed with the day-to-day demands of child rearing. Her father was a self-absorbed, unavailable workaholic traditional father who owned his own successful construction business. In one session, Ruth Ann recalled deciding to be so grown-up and self-sufficient that she could sew her own clothes at age ten. It was essential to her that she need no one. Because it is hopeless to expect people to change deeply ingrained patterns by sheer dint of will, I needed to help Ruth Ann understand the roots of her behavior before she would have the option to do otherwise and the ability to sustain that change. Ruth Ann opened one particularly poignant session with the following confession.

Ruth Ann: I want to work with this feeling of unimportance that I have. It just cuts me like a knife.

Beth: Tell me more of what that is like.

Ruth Ann: I always knew [my parents] loved me and cared about me, but they didn't know how to talk. So I was just alone to grow up. I always felt like a grown-up trapped in a kid's body. I had no childhood. I remember no carefree feelings about childhood at all. *(Tears well in her eyes)*

Beth: Do you know what your tears are?

Ruth Ann: A flood of things! I always knew that my dad wanted boys. So I made the decision to be the boy he never had.

Beth: How did you do that?

Ruth Ann: My dad had a construction business, so I'd run bulldozers and front-end loaders. I just always figured that God made a mistake—that I was supposed to be a boy. I looked at women as weak, and my dad was very powerful. So I wasn't going to be anybody's wife!

Beth: What drew you to going to work with your dad?

Ruth Ann: It was a way to be with him. It was a way to get subtle attention, even if it wasn't from him, if it was from the people who worked with him. So it just cuts me like a knife when Duane ignores me. And I usually get mad or just stuff it, ignore it. But then all the old times I've been ignored come crashing in on me, and it's like a thousand times all at once. It's that deep wound. How do I unload this? I'm just so bitter. I'm right where I was [with Duane]; I've never really forgiven him. And he has improved, so am I sabotaging my success? I just know that my reaction is too out of proportion.

Desperate to have a relationship with her father, Ruth Ann twisted herself like a pretzel to get his attention. Even though it scarcely worked, the crumbs of regard she got from him and his employees were all she could scrape together. These shaped her development very differently from most females as she identified with his masculinity and internalized it in an attempt to please him. However, her choice to marry created three important dynamics for which she had not bargained. One, she did not know how to be a wife. Two, being a wife stirred up powerful crosscurrents of emotions that she was not expecting. Conflicting parts of herself that she had managed to silence began to demand expression in intimate moments with Duane and as she mothered their children. And three, her masculine style was threatening to Duane and his masculinity, despite his protestations to the contrary. Their marriage had reached a stalemate, because each had become half persons, cardboard characters that made them mere caricatures of a woman and a man. They needed to renegotiate a contract that would allow both partners to develop both sides of their personalities. However, this change, too, was a very threatening prospect.

Father Loss: A Family's Estate

Unless the blueprint is changed, the legacy of unresolved father loss becomes part of the estate handed down from one generation to the next. In order for men to become more loving and available parents and partners themselves, they first must acknowledge their own feelings and their need for connection, instead of denying these in the service of being "real men." And in order for women to break self-destructive patterns fueled by low self-esteem, such as perennially seeking emotionally unavailable men so they can duplicate the relationship with their inaccessible father, they also need to be able to acknowledge their feelings, wants and needs. Doing so is not selfish; in fact, it is selfish *not* to do so. When people develop defensiveness to deny such expressions of their humanness, it renders them unavailable to connect with others. *Both women and men first need to face the emptiness created by their life-long loneliness for genuine connection, particularly with their father.* And it goes without saying that this recognition must be from the heart, and not merely a detached, intellectual observation. That is, they must fully face their own father hunger. Only then will men's tendencies to feel and to act like grown-up little boys and women's attractions to these Peter Pans begin to change. Only then will women's dependency no longer be helplessness and will men not be chosen because they pander to her ineptness. When this happens, the pattern handed down from generations in an ever-widening swath of dysfunction can begin to be altered and people can hope to become solid links in their broken family chain. Perhaps a client of mine, a father of three in his late thirties who worked diligently to reverse the legacy of indifference he inherited from his father, stated it best. "It's like [my wife] and I are doing the emotional version of the immigrants: 'By God, my kids are gonna go to school, and they aren't gonna live in dirt houses!'" he said.

The saddest, most insidious implication of unresolved father loss is that for most, the loss now becomes unconscious, and is therefore unnamed and unknowable. And what is unknowable often hurts people because it is experienced as a burden on some level. Then, the father's disappearance becomes more of an erasure than a going away. A child's inability to know, to name and to incorporate a parent's wounds into a world that makes sense can become crippling, even when the source remains mysterious.

In order to understand how father loss affects people, it is important to place it in the context of women's and men's socialization. Because, in addition to unique factors in people's family of origin, exactly how father hunger affects them depends primarily on whether they are male or female. Their sex, to a greater or lesser degree, will govern how they learn to deal with emotions, problems and needs. In as much as females and males in our culture are socialized so differently, each can be expected to respond in contrasting ways, especially to emotionally charged situations. Grounded in this basic understanding of the effects of socialization on women and men, we can consider the kindling effect of socialization on father loss.

Societal Expectations for Men and Women

While generalizations, of course, all have exceptions, it is useful to understand the general rule in order to put anomalies in context. Although members of each sex get additional compelling socialized messages to which they must adapt or pay, those listed are the biggest contributors to father hunger.

What Makes a "Good" Man: Societal Expectations for Men

1. Anger is the one emotion that is acceptable for men. Despite this, the expression of strong emotions is to be avoided by men because of the fear that emotionality

will trigger anger, when they get aroused, that could result in their losing control of themselves.

2. Men show their love by fixing and doing.

3. Men are supposed to be producers and to fix situations and people because their masculinity depends on it. They tend to feel like failures when they cannot succeed in these areas.

4. When men can't fix, they usually get angry and convey the message that the person having the problem should stop having it so they themselves don't feel inadequate.

5. Men tend to avoid emotional conversations because they think there is nothing they can fix. Or they make matters worse when they compulsively try to fix the situation and solve the problem instead of listening.

6. When men need reassurance, they tend to withdraw and feel comforted by protecting themselves.

7. Men prefer to be intimate by doing something together.

8. Men are socialized to be in control, to be the "lone wolf" and "lead horse." They feel like failures when they are not.

9. Men are socialized to compete directly, so they like to be right, to be in charge and to win.

10. In conversation, when men feel threatened or afraid, they try to get the conversation out of the heart and into the head. This is a defense against the fear that the conversation will be transacted on a level where they have no control of themselves, the interaction or the relationship.

11. Men are goal-oriented, so they express themselves best when there is a focus for conversation. When they begin a thought, they like to complete it and feel frustrated or get sidetracked when they can't.

12. Men are solution-oriented, so they tend to internalize their thought processes and only communicate end results.

13. Men believe that when women need to think out loud, they talk too much.

14. Men are expected to deny their dependency needs.

15. Men are taught to exert power in order to be "real" men and that their personal power comes from being autonomous.

What Makes a "Good" Woman: Societal Expectations for Women

1. Anger is the one emotion that women are socialized to believe is unacceptable. So the appropriate expression of anger and assertion often are difficult for them to learn.

2. Women are given the message from birth that they are to be "nice" at all costs. Because anger in women is considered "not nice," women often become controlling and passive-aggressive so they don't seem to be angry or not nice.

3. Women are taught to deal with men indirectly and often become manipulative or passive-aggressive as a result.

4. Women must compete indirectly because nice girls are not supposed to be competitive. So they gossip and are catty instead.

5. Women are process-oriented, so they tend to think out loud.

6. Women are socialized to emphasize relationships and feel like failures when they are unsuccessful in them.

7. Women believe that intimacy requires talking.

8. When women are afraid, they reach out to others and seek to move closer to others to feel reassured.

9. When women feel anxious or self-conscious, they release their tension by talking.

10. Women are socialized to dislike their own bodies and thus develop excessive concern about them.

11. Because women are relationally oriented, they tend to be highly sensitive to and intuitive about relational data, such as nonverbal cues, tone of voice and posture. As a result, they often feel rejected for subtle or imagined reasons.

12. Women are taught to put others' needs ahead of theirs, especially in relationships.

13. Women show their love by nurturing and caretaking.

14. Women are socialized to be dependent.

15. Women are taught to deny their power in order to be "real" women and that their power is in alliance and connection with others.

Socialization and Father Hunger

As Robert Moore and Douglas Gillette wrote, "Ours is an age of personal- and gender-identity chaos."[1] In examining the impact of this gender-related chaos in creating father hunger, there are three elements to consider. The first is how a father's own socialization serves as a backdrop and often interferes with his being emotionally and actually available for his children. The second is the particular risks for sons from inaccessible fathers. The third is the unique way daughters are impacted by unknowing, insensitive or absent fathers.

Fathers Are Socialized Males, Too

Father hunger has been around for a long time, particularly since the Industrial Revolution in the 1800s, when fathers left home to go to work in factories. However, the agony it creates has only recently begun to get the meaningful attention it deserves. Psychiatrist and family therapist Frank Pittman wrote:

> For a couple of hundred years now each generation of fathers has passed on less to his sons. Not just less power, but less wisdom, and less love. We have finally reached a point where most fathers are largely irrelevant in the lives of their sons. The baby has been thrown out with the bath water, and the pater has been dismissed with the patriarchy. Everyone seems to be floundering around not knowing what to do with men or with their problematic and disoriented masculinity.[2]

And although Pittman's book is about fathers and sons, I am certain that he would agree that sons are not alone in getting less than they need from their fathers. As Pittman states, "In a scant two hundred years, in some families in a scant two generations, we've gone from a toxic overdose of fathering to a fatal deficiency."[3]

Fathers avoid emotional connections with their children for many reasons. In part, because of the lack of emotional connection with their own fathers, many men feel defective.

So they hide their shame by resisting any genuinely intimate connection. Appropriate intimacy even with their children seems too great a risk of exposure for many. Consequently the hidden shame they often deliver to their children is, "I am not really able to hold the attention of those I love."[4] Because they themselves feel this way, their children acquire this baggage as well. Fathers are the first men in their children's lives and their strongest vision of masculinity. Their relationship with their children will form the template for all other relationships with men, as we will see in the next chapter.

According to Bryan Strong and Christine DeVault:

> When we speak of mothering a child, everyone knows what we mean: nurturing, caring for, feeding, diapering, soothing and loving. But the meaning of fathering is quite different. Fathering a child need take no more than a few minutes if we understand it in its traditional sense, that is impregnating the mother. Nurturant behavior by a father toward his child has not typically been referred to as fathering.[5]

The sage and beloved Dr. Spock, in his original version of *Baby and Child Care*, published in 1945, voiced the tenor of the time when he wrote, "A man can be a warm father and a real man at the same time. . . . Of course I don't mean that the father has to give as many bottles or change just as many diapers as the mother, but it's fine for him to do these things occasionally. He might make the formula on Sunday."[6] If this were state-of-the-art advice for parents in the era in which many of us or our parents were children, it is little wonder that father hunger exists even for those lucky enough to be able to have their fathers close enough for daily interaction! Since the early

1960s, research has documented the small amount of time fathers typically spend with their children. When fathers live in the home with their children, often their interaction with them typically has been much more limited than it has been with the mother. For instance, in one study in 1971, Rebelsky and Hanks found that fathers interacted with their infants an average of 37.7 seconds per day.[7] A study by Fischman done in 1986 found fathers averaged eight minutes per day with their children on weekdays and fourteen minutes per day on weekends.[8] Although more and more fathers are involved in the pregnancy and birthing process, it is not clear that this greater involvement will translate into increased participation throughout the child's life.

In contrast to the prevailing view of the Ozzie and Harriet generation, in this era of liberation from rigid sex-role pre-scriptions, many men view attachments as paralyzing entrap-ments. Many men believe that caring inevitably will lead to entrapment. These men view attachment and caregiving as, at best, way stations for those who have not achieved "mature" goals of separateness and independence. For those who look at fatherhood from this perspective, it would be no surprise that intimate relationships with both children and their moth-ers are to be avoided at all costs. One might speculate about the sort of relationship they had with their father. For many of these men, their major accomplishments in life are making a baby in their own image that they don't have to rear and mark-ing a woman as their conquest. Sometimes babies make babies. But other times, in accordance with our culture's acceptance of the shrinking father, this behavior is not just the province of teenagers. Being a touch-and-go father is becom-ing increasingly acceptable for men of all ages.

Fathers and Sons: Anointed As Man Enough

How do emotionally or physically absent fathers affect men? It is easiest to consider this by discussing what knowledge of and contact with fathers does *for* boys.

Perhaps the single most significant contribution that fathers make to their sons is to anoint them "man enough." Males may try to be true men, but if they had "fathers who ran out on the job,"[9] they likely will always feel like masculine impostors. Then, they become "amateur males . . . [because] without the experience of learning to be a man and a father by hanging around with one of them, boys who want to become men have to guess at what men are like."[10]

One participant in a men's group I ran spoke eloquently about his being intimidated in the presence of other men. Bob, age forty, had been abandoned by his father at the time of the parents' divorce, when the boy was eight. Cowed by males after that, he had always hung around women because they seemed safer, even choosing a career considered by most to be "women's work." When he sat mute for the entire first men's group, I began to question my judgment. Had I blundered by putting him in a men's group at all, I fretted, especially one with so many high-powered men? Would he be too overwhelmed to gain anything from the experience? The worst question was, would the group experience harm him somehow? I was relieved when he began the second group meeting with the following elegantly simple explanation for his silence the previous meeting: "I felt like I was sitting in a room full of fathers last time. That's why I couldn't talk!"

Although no one can anoint a son man enough the way a father can, a substitute is the company of men with whom to practice being a man, to be appreciated and with whom to bond. For many, the closest they can come to being parented is having grown-up men who lovingly don't expect too much and who "share the shame of never being man enough."[11] This allows men finally to learn the elegantly simple paradox that it is dependence that makes independence possible.

Since boys both learn how to be men and that they are man enough by hanging around their fathers, men who are robbed of that experience often never feel comfortable with what it means to be a man. And nowhere does this show up more than when it is time to go out into the world and operate as competent men. Those who must guess at what it is to be a man are left with the grotesque models of Rambo and the Terminator to use as guides. And then, of course, they pass on, either directly or in their abdication, that cardboard-character hypermasculine role model to their sons. And often, sons are left stranded this way by their fathers because to raise their sons, fathers have to confront their own feelings of inadequacy that stir as they strive both to live up to and to model their ideals of manhood. These internal conflicts become particularly poignant as they observe what their sons must contend with in becoming men.

Men who did not have fathers to initiate them into manhood become very dependent on women to take care of them and even to define them. Yet, in light of the prohibition against men having needs, men who find themselves needing women are frightened and shameful. Closeness to women also can stir up boys' conflict between needing protection and the competing need for independence. This, of course, usually results in boys feeling less manly. Needing their mother is a consolation prize that pales by comparison to the jackpot of closeness with their father. Terry explained this phenomenon simply to his parents in a family-of-origin session I ran when he finally confessed how much he has needed his dad and how little of him he got. While thanking his mother for all she had done, he said simply to his father, "But Mom's not a guy!" The following session, Terry described the multiple ripple effects he already could sense from those four delicious hours of heart-to-heart talking and crying with his father, for the first time in his life.

Terry: I just feel I'm better able to deal with things now.
Beth: How did the session help with that?
Terry: My father admitted that he has had problems.
Beth: How does your father's admission that he's had problems affect you?
Terry: I think his admitting he has problems allows me to cut myself some slack, to not expect myself to be so perfect.
Both: Hallelujah!

A father is the gatekeeper to his son's healthy masculinity. The son begins to feel man enough with his father's help. Then he can come to feel increasingly less ashamed of his own perceived inadequacies and the inevitable difficulties of life.

Sometimes men react with physical violence in a pathetic effort to "prove" that they are real men, to seal off their frightening tender feelings or because their brains are wired to go directly from feeling to acting. Others, because it would be unacceptable any other way, develop physical or emotional symptoms to legitimate being taken care of. Still others become overachievers and workaholics who are insensitive to anyone's needs, including their own, in a pathetic effort to feel competent. Others become philanderers in an attempt to feel like successful men without having to risk their need for a woman or the fear that she'll take control of them. And others still compete in the grown-up economic contests that have replaced adolescent skirmishes about penis size because they must compete to feel alive and man enough. Men who cannot learn healthy competition with their fathers either become ineffectual like Casper Milquetoast or cutthroat like the corporate raider. *Being able to succeed by competing is the priority to men that the need to relate is to women.*

Perhaps the trump card that both underlies and compounds all of the above factors that makes father loss most precarious for men is the prohibition our culture places on the expression of emotions for men. The expression of emotions is the prime prerequisite for moving through and resolving a loss. Because men's socialization prohibits the open expression of feelings for them, men are not only at risk of experiencing father hunger, but also are apt to get stuck on it. As Robert Bly, the poet laureate of the men's movement, said, "Grief is the doorway to a man's feelings. But men don't know what they are grieving about." [12] Sam Keen of *Fire in the Belly* fame put it another way. He wrote simply, "Men have much to mourn before they can be reborn." [13] In sum, while it is imperative for men to grieve, their socialization and their absent fathers conspire against them.

For many, trying to be a good enough man in today's world can seem like a precarious, no-win situation. As Samuel Osherson wrote, being a man today is like learning how to tie your shoelaces all over again. These are not real shoelaces, but ties that bind us to those we love. Men have "to learn all over again how to tie those knots." [14]

Fathers and Daughters:
A Safe Place to Practice Being a Woman

It is not just boys who need contact with their fathers as they search for models who will help them discover who they are. Girls need their fathers, too. Parents don't have to teach their children consciously how to be girls or boys, or how to relate to the opposite sex. Children just follow the examples around them. Yet, for some fathers, the birth of a daughter brings with it a sense of *the other.* And because of this, it can be hard for him to imagine her as an extension of himself and for him to know what to do with her. Because she is the opposite sex, many fathers feel inadequate and therefore ashamed, so they withdraw. At least, however, most daughters are spared the natural tendency toward competitiveness that fathers and sons often experience because of this.

Studies of successful women have found that fathers are very important to their daughters and that women engage in a lifelong process of coming to terms with them.[15] A father's emotionally engaging with his daughter helps shape her confident vision of happiness as an adult, as well as her goals regarding work and love. Fathers are safe men with whom daughters can practice being women. Although most people, and especially women, feel the most treasured when they feel heard, often a father's showing his love by performance suffices *if* she feels valued by him for who she is. This helps her to learn and to come to expect to feel valued by men. A father's affirmation of both his daughter's competence and her femininity are crucial to her ability to realize that she can feel *both* womanly and successful, loving and competent. In fact, Kirk Johnson and Judith Springer Riddle concluded that fathers are crucial to girls' emotional growth.[16]

However, just as fathers sometimes withdraw from their sons in the hope of encouraging their autonomy, many daughters experience their fathers' pulling away from the normal "father-daughter romance"[17] when they reach puberty. Because females tend to internalize and to blame themselves when something goes wrong in a relationship, many girls go into their adolescence believing something is wrong with them if their father is no longer affectionate or close. However, many fathers do this as their effort to prevent any chance that they could become aroused by their daughter's budding womanhood or flooded by their own intense emotions. Other fathers report that their withdrawal is to protect their daughters from feeling confused by her own sexual stirrings. Parenting girls can be especially challenging for fathers because fathers' experience and skills are usually so different from what a daughter needs.

And these girls are the lucky ones! At least they have had a relationship with their father, with whom they could try on being a woman until puberty, when he protectively pulls back. Other women are not so fortunate. Too often, a father's emphasis on autonomy and the denial of feelings renders him oblivious to her needs. But since her socialization as a female inclines her toward relationships and emotions, she likely will feel stranded and even rejected if her father continues to emphasize his needs for separation rather than her needs for connection. So girls often intuit, as I did, that in order to have a personal connection with their father, they must accept it on his terms or not at all. This demand, of course, seldom is stated overtly or consciously acknowledged. But because girls are socialized that their growth is in connection and that relationship failures are their failures, many girls trade their own reality and needs for his long before they are mature enough to grasp the full meaning of the choice. And because a girl's relationship with her father provides an unconscious blueprint for all of her relationships with men, alienating herself from her own reality in the service of the relationship becomes a way of relating to men. However, because such relationships are a one-way street, genuine intimacy is not possible. Left to her own devices, she inevitably will bring these patterns into her adult relationships. This, of course, provides the incubating conditions for co-dependent, enabling women. In short, father hunger for too many women knocks the balance between self and other out of whack. Craving a relationship with a special man, they find themselves doing anything to please and, therefore, finally to win approval. Or they go to the other extreme of being more "macho" than men, as Ruth Ann did, denying all feelings or need for connection.

Just as there are for men, there are numerous symptoms that manifest when women try to cope with father loss without being able to acknowledge it.

One is the female version of Rambo: "Superwoman." She does everything perfectly, has it all together, is tough and needs no one. Emotional connectedness is usually a woman's strongest drive, so taking care of others easily can become more important than taking care of herself. And she, of course, does it all without expecting much in return. As a result, she often is attracted to little boys masquerading as grown men, whom she can mother, control and not need because it is not safe to do so. This has the added "benefit" of allowing her to continue to deny her own needs in the service of her poor, helpless family and her grown-up little boy. Women who are *really* Superwomen expect themselves to do everything a man can do in addition to everything a woman can do.

Another often deadly symptom is a fixation on personal appearance. Margo Maine wrote, "Appearance has a unique meaning for women, reflecting both their connections with themselves and with others. Women know they can please others through their bodies."[18] This can be a blessing because it gives women power, particularly in interactions with men. But it also can be a curse. Maine goes on to say, "Although the way to a man's heart may be through his stomach, as tradition dictates, the way to get male attention is to be thin."[19] This, of course, sets women up for eating disorders of all kinds as they both try to control their father hunger and their bodies, and still fulfill society's dictates. Thus, many young women are willing to starve themselves in an ill-fated effort to get understanding, affection and love from a man. Of course, it never works because they never feel genuinely accepted for who they are. Failing that, these young women must settle for attention. Other women gave up on attracting men with their bodies because they could not get their father's attention. These people develop the eating disorder of obesity to push people away while they attempt to quell their voracious hunger. To either type of woman, their bodies can become protective cocoons as well as arenas to feel some control since likely they have felt little ability to genuinely influence their father.

Teen pregnancy and/or early marriage are still other ways girls both attempt to express their power in the world and to try to fill their hunger for love. The fantasy is that maybe now, someone will always love them, be there for them and not leave. The first cousin to this is sexual promiscuity. What better way to anesthetize depression; to attempt to fill the empty space inside; to draw men in while casting them aside; to be touched in ways that masquerade as love; and to express anger at and mistrust of men all in one fell swoop! Yet, we as a society pay dearly for this "solution." Teen pregnancy costs us $2.9 billion every year, and sons of these mothers are three times more likely to end up in prison.[20] The statistic doesn't even begin to describe the human toll behind these numbers.

Physical problems of all kinds sometimes may be reflective of unresolved father hunger. With a woman's tendency to internalize so she can continue to be pleasing and to serve as the caretaker, she is at risk for developing physical problems. If she experiences unresolved father hunger, she may be hoping, however unconsciously, that her illness will provide the opportunity for her father to come to her rescue—or at least to come see her. As we saw in chapter 3 with Cara, a child's illness or dysfunction can serve the function of getting a peripheral, preoccupied father involved in the family. When a daughter sends her emotions into her body and becomes ill, she may unconsciously believe that she has found the only safe container for her feelings. With all of this secondary gain at stake, once again she steps up to the line to sacrifice herself in the service of a relationship, sometimes even making the ultimate sacrifice.

Because men are programmed into separation and isolation and, as a result, often have problems with emotional intimacy, few that are like this know how to be dads. In contrast, females are pressured to put others first, and therefore, they have difficulty separating and individuating. Thus, they need to feel connected and probably will not feel satisfied or filled up by a peripheral father. Because of their socialization, girls seem to get an extra dose of egocentrism, and thus guilt becomes the hallmark of the female psyche the way isolation is for males. Men learn to ignore feelings, and women learn to obsess about how they must have caused the underlying problem. Women stay in relationships too long and at their own expense because their father's literal or emotional absence creates a situation that is ripe for the masochism.

Finally, because girls learn how to trade on their looks and because fathers are providers, sometimes fathers try to make contact with their daughters by buying them. Being the economic provider is not a sufficient basis for an emotionally fulfilling relationship, but often daughters feel guilty about wanting more and exploitative about getting what they get. Their father may tell them that they are too demanding if they want more of a personal nature from him. So they usually feel guilty and begin to deny these needs, trying to go along to get along.

Since a daughter's relationship with her father will be the prototype for her relationships with all other men, her father hunger will color the rest of her life, particularly if she does not take steps to resolve it. Healthy personal identity for anyone requires a feeling of mastery and independence in the world. For women, however, this can be a tricky proposition since pleasing others is a necessary ingredient to their identities. Girls who grow up feeling loved and respected by their father generate a sense of personal power that enables them to make and stand by tough decisions. They are able to balance the needs of self with the demands of others. Those who don't enjoy or haven't enjoyed this kind of connection with their father will have varying degrees of difficulty achieving this equilibrium.

Whether they know it or not, fathers are a significant influence on their daughter's acceptance or rejection of sexuality, body image, eating and health habits, and general self-esteem.

Fathers who know how to stay close to daughters in accordance with their developmental needs make an invaluable contribution to their daughter's maturity. Yet, the sad fact is that many fathers seem less invested in their daughters than in their sons. For example, fathers with sons are less likely to divorce than fathers of daughters.[21] It appears that if fathers are unclear as to their importance in the lives of their sons, many are virtually oblivious about their place in their daughters' lives.

Similarities in the Ways Men and Women Experience Father Loss

It would be a mistake to conclude that both the experience of and impact on each sex from unavailable fathers are totally different. However, even in the similarities, the ways in which each sex deals with each painful outcome usually are qualitatively different and dependent primarily on the differences in socialization of each.

Decreased Self-Esteem

When children are deprived of knowledge of and contact with their father, especially if that deprivation is the parent's choice, it is difficult for those children to feel the same sense of wholeness and worthiness that children with hands-on fathers do. For men, this becomes the most apparent when it is time for them to go out into the world and make their way as a competent adult. It is hard for them to feel man enough. So either they rarely venture out, or they overcompensate and develop a hypermasculine persona. Women's difficulty with developing self-esteem and with believing in themselves usually shows up in problems with relationships and in difficulties with autonomy and competence. Many either can't find someone to love, or they love too much and at their own expense. They also are confused about how to be both competent and a lover at the same time.

Fear of Abandonment

Already actually abandoned by their father (and perhaps emotionally so by an overburdened mother trying to be both parents), there is nothing hypothetical for these people about what abandonment is like. It seems all too normal. Men protect themselves from this by exaggerating traits that our culture typically has required of men: that they be strong, rational, intellectual and in control. This allows them to contain their emotions and to remain safely detached so they can leave first. Women cope with this by embroidering the messages they already get from our culture. Because most emotions are acceptable and relationships are expected for women, they either become clinging vines to ensure they will be taken care of, or they become drill sergeants to keep the upper hand. Both of these adaptations keep vulnerable feelings and intimate others at bay. Both types of women have figured out how not to be alone; but neither knows very well how to be together because togetherness makes the specter of being abandoned again too terrifying.

Exaggerated Fears of Being Alone

Being abandoned by a parent also compromises a child's orderly separation and individuation process. Therefore, these children have great difficulty learning to stand alone and be alone. They often make the common mistake of assuming that being alone and lonely are the same. Men cope with their fears by mechanisms that usually involve frenetic activity. They work out and work, feign fear of nothing, excessively use chemicals, and make conquests of women so they don't have to be alone—but they don't have to be together, either. Because of women's emphasis on relationship and connection, and because these women already feel abandoned by their fathers, they often go to great lengths to ensure that they won't be abandoned by another man. So they either stay too long in destructive relationships or refuse to invest in them, becoming like the black widow. Often, the only constant companions (they can trust that won't leave) are food, chemicals, cigarettes, children or excessive concern about these.

Feeling Shame

People who have been wounded generally have difficulty revealing that wound to anyone or even allowing themselves to see and feel it. Men struggle with how to connect with people—and yet with how to get away from them. Their avoidance of intimate moments allows them to sidestep the wounded parts of themselves that they devalue. It also allows them to avoid the shame that is stirred up when they feel vulnerable. Women's shame generally relates to not feeling valued by others and, therefore, not valuable. And yet, often they are starved for affection. This makes them good candidates for codependent relationships as they give up their own needs in the service of others or for having extramarital affairs in which they receive only crumbs. These coping styles have the added "benefit" of masking their own longing and neediness of which they feel ashamed.

Counterdependence

When people do not have firsthand knowledge that those whom they need will be there for them and will stay, they often protect themselves from getting hurt again by acting as if they don't need anyone. Men like this often appear to be the strong, silent type. This serves to contain emotions and needs that they fear would overpower them. They can't get out from behind their protective wall, but no one can get in, either. Women's typical way of being counterdependent and feeling strong is surreptitiously to get their own needs met by meeting someone else's. These people become great enablers and caretakers. Or they develop a persona around a hard, impenetrable shell.

Problems Managing Emotions

People who have experienced a trauma, particularly one early in their lives, often fluctuate between effusive emotions and being shut down. This is particularly risky for men because our culture expects them to be strong and silent, as if those words were synonyms. Some women, on the other hand, tend toward effusive emotions and have difficulty being rational when their emotions are stirred. Both make the mistake of assuming that it is impossible to think and feel at the same time. So, typically, he thinks, and she feels. And then, neither can connect. This leaves both members of the couple half people.

Problems with Anger

Anger is a natural response to feeling abandoned. However, because anger is the primary acceptable emotion for men, they often display it only so they can hide behind it or feel powerful because of it. The ultimate form of this is murdering women for abandoning them. That way, they can possess their women forever, and no one else can have them. Women's problem generally is the opposite. They are much more likely to turn their anger inward. When they do, depression, eating disorders, substance abuse and other self-defeating, self-destructive behaviors result.

Need to Control

There are both subtle and blatant ways to be controlling. But whichever manifestation people choose, the goal is to attempt to cover or at least to manage fear. People who are controlling are afraid of letting someone become close and of being abandoned. These people often are relationship terrorists. Because men are expected to be fixers and in charge, they often become blatantly controlling ("It's my way or the high way!") or subtly so by being everyone's American Express card. Women's ways of controlling generally are masked, because of their socialization to be nice at all costs. So they tend to control by such tactics as manipulating people, using guilt, pouting, withdrawal of love and passive aggression. Both men and women can control by helplessness, which paradoxically is a very powerful tactic.

Problems with Trusting

This is the sum total of the previously listed manifestations of father hunger. And it is the ultimate outcome.

Undoubtedly this is only a partial list and not meant to be exhaustive. Readers are encouraged to add to it.

A Final Word

Of course, the signs and symptoms that are emblematic of father loss also can derive from other experiences. For example, an adolescent at this juncture in our cultural evolution is being bombarded daily by messages that undermine the influence of even the most loving and competent parents, as Mary Pipher states in her bestseller *Reviving Ophelia*.[22] So it is important not to jump to conclusions, blaming fathers automatically or condemning either beleaguered parent, for that matter. Perhaps a more helpful way to think about the earmarks offered in this book is to see them as invitations for further exploration. For example, although low self-esteem for children also may arise from ongoing problems with gaining peer acceptance, one might ponder the degree to which their father's presence or absence either helps inoculate the children or exacerbate their loneliness and pain.

It is difficult for anyone to be vulnerable unless there is a caring receiver of those emotions. Yet, too often, one of a child's two primary attachment figures is totally absent, appears to be disinterested or is otherwise unavailable. When fathers are disengaged, their detachment undermines their children in many ways, the most important of which is in their ability to love, feel loved and feel worthy of both.

References

1. Robert Moore and Douglas Gillette, *King, Warrior, Magician, Lover: Rediscovering the Archetypes of the Mature Masculine* (San Francisco: Harper San Francisco, 1990), 102.

2. Frank Pittman, *Man Enough: Fathers, Sons, and the Search for Masculinity* (New York: G. P. Putnam's Sons, 1993), 121.

3. Ibid., 134.

4. Osherson, *Wrestling with Love*, (New York: Columbine Fawcett, 1992), 68.

5. Bryan Strong and Christine DeVault, *The Marriage and Family Experience*, 5th ed. (St. Paul: West Publishing, 1992), 334.

6. Benjamin Spock, *Baby and Child Care* (New York: Pocket Books, 1945), 97.

7. Strong and DeVault, *Marriage and Family Experience,* 334.

8. Ibid., 334.

9. Pittman, *Man Enough,* 14.

10. Ibid., 19.

11. Ibid., 176.

12. Robert Bly, *A Gathering of Men: With Bill Moyers and Robert Bly* (New York: Mystic Fire Video, 1989).

13. Sam Keen, *Fire in the Belly: On Being a Man* (New York: Bantam, 1991), 136.

14. Osherson, *Wrestling with Love* (New York: Columbine Fawcett, 1992), 351.

15. Lora Tessman, "Fathers and Daughters: Early Tones, Later Echoes," in S. Cath, A. Gurwitt, and L. Gunsberg, *Fathers and Their Families.*

16. Kirk Johnson and Judith Springer Riddle, "Fathers Are Crucial to Girls' Emotional Growth," *Arizona Daily Star,* 3 February 1998: B1.

17. Osherson, *Wrestling with Love* (New York: Columbine Fawcett, 1992), 246.

18. Margo Maine, *Father Hunger: Fathers, Daughters, and Food* (Carlsbad, Calif.: Gurze Books, 1991), 63.

19. Ibid., 69

20. NBC's *The Today Show,* 14 June 1996.

21. Strong and Christine DeVault, *The Marriage and Family Experience,* 5th ed. (St. Paul: West Publishing, 1992), 518.

22. Mary Pipher, *Reviving Ophelia* (San Francisco: Harper San Francisco, 1996), 23.

6

Come Here, Go Away: Father Loss and Intimate Relationships

Intimacy requires
courage because risk is inescapable.
We cannot know at the outset how
the relationship will affect us.

—Rollo May
The Courage to Create

How can events so far in the past and seemingly so unrelated to a couple's day-to-day lives have such a profound impact? Perhaps the two most significant answers to this question relate to the choice of partner made by those with unresolved father loss and the relationship dynamics those people subsequently develop.

Loss has the extraordinary capacity of affecting the development of individuals. As I discussed, healthy relationships are formed and maintained by two healthy individuals. Yet, loss ultimately can arrest individuals' development, leaving them defensively cocooned and emotional children. This, in turn, jeopardizes their intimate relationships. And when the loss is chronic and unresolved, regardless of its source, it is even more precarious than one that is resolved at the time it occurs. Yet, when a loss has transpired and involved someone as significant as an emotionally or actually unavailable father, the effect that the loss has on the capacity of the individual to develop is seldom recognized. And, of course, only when the loss is acknowledged can it be dealt with appropriately and finished. Otherwise, its capacity to perpetuate pain cannot be contained. Further, when the acute phase of grieving has passed and the pain has aged, the pain frequently combines with other unresolved feelings or "emotional debts," as psychiatrist David Viscott calls them.[1] This combination compounds the effects of each. Furthermore, unless the loss is addressed and resolved, the chronically grieved can expect to have great difficulty being genuinely emotionally available to anyone. In this chapter, we will see why that is.

Ted and Penny: "How Can We Be Close When We Need to Keep Our Distance?"

Ted initially was referred to me by his family physician, who was becoming increasingly concerned about Ted's depression and suicidal thoughts. I recognized his name from his first message because he was something of a regional celebrity as a politician. Although he initially expected to work with me individually, because he was married, I requested that his wife join us. Surely she was being affected by his moods. And I needed to make certain that she wasn't unwittingly feeding into them. Secretly, I also suspected that she had her own issues that reflected his somehow. Both willingly agreed to my suggestion, with Ted seeming particularly relieved that he did not have to fix this problem himself.

When I first met Ted, he seemed almost crumpled in his withdrawal. He was extremely self-critical, despite the popularity evidenced by his multiple awards and re-elections. In describing what he was experiencing, he referred to being in a "black hole" and kept saying, "There are no colors." Depression is difficult enough for anyone to experience, but for Ted, it was extremely precarious. Because his profession required that he be "on" at all times, if his black moods did not result in actual suicide, they had the potential to cause professional suicide. It was no surprise that his acute awareness of this potential only worsened the ever-darkening storm clouds inside and around him. And, of course, it hampered his effectiveness on the job as well.

Ted was a forty-five-year-old yuppie married to his college sweetheart for twenty-three years. They shared two preschool children and an active lifestyle fueled by the passion of shared political beliefs. Ted described their marriage as one with which he was generally quite satisfied, except for having less frequent sex than he preferred. Penny spoke with mild disdain of Ted's being "high maintenance" because of his general depression and neediness, but on balance, she reported being happy with the marriage. Because it seemed like the words and the music of their message were congruent, I turned my attention to identifying other factors that might be generating Ted's angst. And it did not take much probing to discover what they were.

Ted had grown up with a policeman father who generally was absent because of working evening or night shifts. And the father was emotionally unavailable as well. When he was home, the father either was sleeping or seething about department politics or the ghastly events he saw on his beat.

In addition to these factors that conspired to draw father and son apart, the father's childhood rendered him more unavailable to Ted, through no fault of his own. Ted's grandmother had died in childbirth while bearing Ted's father. And because the grandfather believed that the death of his wife resulted from his pushing her in a fight they had immediately before she went into labor, he could not live with his guilt. So he killed himself—on the child's first birthday. From there, Ted's father was shuffled from pillar to post until a childless aunt and uncle finally took pity on him and took him in. However, already in their fifties at the time, their main contribution to the child's life was providing him stability, three meals a day, a bed and a bicycle. Although this certainly was better than the alternatives, it was a loveless household. To compound matters, two sisters of Ted's father also committed suicide out of their own anger and despair about being orphaned. So, from infancy on, for an intricate set of reasons, Ted's father had felt worthless, joyless, depressed, wrong and in constant need to atone for his original sins of his parents' deaths.

Thus, Ted's father had scant emotional supplies to give his son because he got few from his surrogate father and even fewer from his own father. But what Ted did get from his father was a tendency toward depression, feelings of worthlessness and a craving to please. Heredity and environment conspired against both Ted and his father. While his drive to please was a major factor in Ted's professional success, it also was a ticking time bomb waiting to implode into depression.

Just Ted's age, Penny eclipsed a promising career fresh out of college to follow Ted in his work. Then she quit her career entirely when they had children. She was as understated and unadorned as Ted was sparkling and spirited. So each person's style provided a balance for the other's. Although both were proud of the longevity of and their commitment to their marriage, when they were really honest with themselves, each knew that something was missing. To put it simply, they had trouble connecting emotionally, and Ted's distancing by depression certainly was a factor as was Penny's distancing by perfectionism.

Penny's family, if one didn't look too closely, seemed like the all-American model. In fact, Penny had convinced herself that it was. All through high school and college, she had been a straight-A student, cheerleader, and athlete. The middle child in a large family growing up in a small Midwestern town, she felt she needed to be perfect to be noticed. Being perfect also helped her to atone for her family's shameful secret of her father's alcoholism. As Robert Ackerman wrote in his book *Perfect Daughters: Adult Children of Alcoholics,* "Developing a sense of personal identity becomes over-shadowed by a negative family identity."[2] Her father, being a traveling salesman, compounded her difficulty by being on the road five nights a week and not offering any nurturance. She concluded that her only chance to get his attention was to be perfect, which, by adolescence, she had honed to a fine art. In addition, being left in the care of a mother who was chronically overburdened by the demands of rearing many children and emotionally drained by an absent, alcoholic spouse meant that few of Penny's needs were met by her mother on a consistent basis. Moreover, both parents' ethnic backgrounds made them stoic, dismissive and even derisive of needs. They viewed them as weaknesses and taught Penny to believe the same. So Penny learned how to surrender her needs in the service of the family.

Penny unintentionally and unconsciously learned many childhood lessons in her family from growing up with one parent who was absent and alcoholic, and the other who was overwhelmed and angry. She learned from her father's repeated episodes of stumbling home drunk late at night, lurching down the steps to sleep alone in the basement, falling down in a sodden heap and bleeding, and her parents' loud fights and cold wars. From watching their behavior Penny learned to act in ways that Robert Ackerman wrote about:

- If I can control everything, I can keep my family from becoming upset.
- If I please everyone, everyone will be happy.
- It is my fault, and I am to blame when trouble occurs.
- Those who love you the most are those who cause you the most pain.
- If I don't get too close emotionally, you cannot hurt me.
- It is my responsibility to ensure that everyone in the family gets along with each other.
- Take care of others first.
- Nothing is wrong, but I don't feel right.
- Expressing anger is not appropriate.
- Something is missing in my life.

- I'm unique; so is my family.
- I can deny anything.
- I am not a good person.
- I am responsible for the success of a relationship.
- For something to be acceptable, it must be perfect.[3]

With strictures such as these in her head and covertly governing her behavior, it is little wonder that she kept her distance from Ted lest he see the imperfections she shamefully knew she had. It is also no surprise that she distanced from Ted, particularly when he was depressed, so her helplessness wouldn't make her feel like a failure and so that she would not feel abandoned by him as he turned inward. Her unconscious mind reasoned that if she kept her distance, then it wouldn't hurt when Ted's depression and self-absorption took her away from him, because she'd have gone first. This gave her the illusion of control. Besides, she saw his depression as weakness, and she recoiled from both it and him when he was in that state. Of course, these defensive maneuvers left Ted feeling rejected and contributed to his spiral of darkening moods because of his old, familiar feelings of abandonment. Then Ted's depression triggered Penny's impulse to distance from him and from herself, which depressed him further, and the cycle continued. This dance left each of them feeling bereft and alone but unable to talk about it.

What was the role of each person's father hunger in their distance? And how could I help each of them resolve their losses and thereby remove the barrier they had created?

Unresolved Father Loss Becomes Braided into Relationship Dynamics

Unresolved loss creates a barrier to intimacy. Because all individuals help shape their emerging relationship systems, those who have experienced loss mold their relationships around it, paradoxically, to stay away from it. This invisible and impenetrable barrier can be erected in any meaningful relationship: between parents and children, within couples, among friends, and even between therapists and clients. However, nowhere is this block more apparent than in spousal relationships. Perhaps nowhere do its aftereffects have more potential to stifle intimacy than when a partner has been abandoned by a parent. One reason is because the potential closeness of a spouse can revive primitive emotions from childhood, even in healthy relationships with people who have experienced no particular trauma. But when people are wounded, sensing or seeing their partner's hurt often sets off reverberations of their own pain. So, chronically grieved people tend to reject the partner who is hurt or needy, thereby increasing their partner's hurt by their self-protection. Otherwise, they fear, the pain they see reflected back to them might overwhelm them. Thus, if they shut down their partner on the pretext of helping the other feel better, it has three self-serving side effects:

- Seeming to proffer a loving act
- Insulating themselves from their own emotions
- Keeping the partner at bay

However, what most whose modus operandi centers on these sorts of defensive maneuvers do not see is that they carry on this way at their own risk.

People who have unresolved relics from the past work consciously and unconsciously to avoid any reminders of those feelings. They may often intuitively feel that the risks inherent in making a vital and close connection with another seem too dangerous and overwhelming to be ventured. So they develop a whole way of relating that attempts to ensure that they won't be hurt again as they were before. They then wallpaper layer upon layer of defenses to keep themselves away from their loss, from any reminders of it or from threats of repeating it. Thus, defending against reemergence of the loss shapes people's way of coping, skews their view of their relationship and of the world, and eventually becomes their entire reality. Thus, unwittingly, they limit their own growth and stifle their relationship in the process.

Do People Choose Partners Consciously?

In a word, no. People don't lie awake at night writing a personals ad or its mental equivalent seeking someone to help them avoid themselves. But if they did, it might go something like this:

> Single, chronically grieved person seeks partner to perpetuate abandonment. Can be emotional or actual. May be married to someone else or not. Ideal if person also needs to avoid closeness because of own abandonment, but any reason will do.

It is as if people with unresolved losses have a Geiger counter that clicks away when they meet someone who will help them replay their old issues. This is for two reasons. One is that abandonment is "normal" for them. And two, since it is familiar, they experience little suspense and some control, however little. On both counts, they know their lines and the steps of their well-choreographed dance. What they don't know is how to act another part. And until the grooves in their psyche that have been created by their original abandonment have been smoothed over by a combination of their new insight and finally experiencing the emotions shelved so long ago, their tendency will be to stay in those old grooves.

Keep Fighting the Same Battle— Or Finally Win the War?

Ever wonder why people keep being attracted to the same type of partner, despite their fervent resolutions not to make the same mistake again? A major dynamic at work when people choose partners is the internal and unconscious pull toward continually repeated patterns they learned in their family of origin, coupled with the intuitive draw toward what is healthy and will promote growth and development. Which attraction will win out depends on the degree to which they consciously understand their motivators. Consider the woman who divorces the alcoholic and marries the workaholic. Or the man who divorces the woman who puts her appearance first, only to marry one who puts the children first. How many times have we all vowed never to be like our parents or to make their mistakes? No matter how problematic, what we observed and internalized from our family of origin seems "normal" and, therefore, right—even if on a conscious level it is obviously wrong for us. In order to be able to acquire the option to do what truly is right for us, we need to understand our own and our family's patterns.

Relationship choice is a complicated business. Many complex factors operate on several levels, most of which are rarely conscious. But when people choose partners to love, they virtually are always intuitively wise on some level. It is merely a matter of figuring out how *genuinely* wise their choice is.

Should people make conscious choices in their relationships? Of course! But that is usually very difficult, if not impossible to do by sheer dint of will, when individuals' core dynamics are rooted in the avoidance of a loss. Most likely, until that loss is resolved, people will stay enmeshed in it. However, resolving the loss allows people to understand the psychic fuel for their problematic behavior and to disconnect the fuel line. Otherwise, they will be consigned to reacting reflexively in knee-jerk fashion. Therefore, the main advantage of attaining this level of understanding is that then, people have choices and some control over their unruly and problematic unconscious programming.

For example, people with unresolved father loss may promise themselves never to be abandoned again by maintaining control, by denying needs and by burying emotions, as Penny did. While that *appears* to work, there is a price. Often, people who feel controlled by them eventually give up on the relationship and leave anyway. Ted's depression was his way of escaping. If we had been unable to change that repetitive pattern, one of two outcomes would have continued to predominate their marriage. Either Ted would have needed to resign himself to depression for a lifetime, or he would eventually have left. Sometimes partners find ways to escape emotionally even if they can't or don't actually leave. Many fed-up partners have affairs in an attempt to get their needs met. So these control freaks are abandoned anyway. In reality, these people, as both Ted and Penny were, are participants in the engineering of their own abandonment.

Women particularly will not tolerate a relationship with this degree of distance and dysfunction, as psychologist Mavis Hetherington's research reveals.[4] She stated that women generally need to be in a *happy* marriage, while for men, *being* married generally suffices. This provides one explanation for why women initiate three-fourths of divorces, and why men remarry sooner after divorce than women. Therefore, it is important, when contemplating relationships, either one's own or those that seem enviable, to have a clear and appropriate definition of what "works" means.

Key Terms Defined

It is important that you clearly understand the meaning of several important terms before we proceed.

Defense: A useful way to think of a defense is that it is a psychic callous that people grow, or a shield that they unconsciously erect, to protect themselves from the pain of being hurt again. People come by their defenses honestly and because they have been hurt. Thus, a rigid defensive pattern both signifies and creates an emotional scar. However, the defense that results can wreak havoc in relationships, even as it provides protection to the individual.

Not all defenses have dangerous consequences; no one would exist for very long without functional defenses. An example is the ability to accept that not everyone will approve of everything you do, or to console yourself in the face of disappointment or embarrassment. However, these same defenses create obvious problems in relationships because they make genuine intimacy difficult, if not impossible. Usually, attempts to eliminate the defense head-on are doomed to failure. Defenses are designed to do a job, and in doing so they can be most resilient. The stubbornness of the defense not to surrender its task is called *resistance*. Unless the trauma that caused the pain that gave rise to the callus is reworked at the source, that original defense will likely remain intact and continue to wreak havoc, even while it protects. Only by removing the pain and reworking the trauma does the defense begin to disappear, thereby allowing the individual the freedom to grow in a healthy fashion. Because this pain has been hidden so well and for so long, finding the offending pain, identifying its source and resolving it often requires the help of a trained professional. But regardless of whether or not people seek professional help, their suffering can be eroded only when they become able to face the truth.

Dynamics: These are one form of a defense. Dynamics are created in a relationship because of both people's defenses. All individuals have dynamics that are formed by their prior experiences, particularly if those experiences were wounding. And both spouses bring their individual dynamics into their marriage to weave marital dynamics. *A dynamic is a motivating or controlling force that operates in a person's life at an unconscious level.* Those dynamics that come from experiences in childhood usually have the most power. However, traumatic adult experiences such as being raped, being divorced or going bankrupt also can shape people's dynamics. Here are five important points to understand about dynamics:

- Everyone has them.
- They usually control or propel behavior.
- They usually operate outside a person's awareness.
- The way to attain genuine control in one's life is to understand those dynamics and to express the emotions embedded in them and that caused them.
- Perhaps the deepest trust in a relationship comes from understanding each other's dynamics and having confidence that this knowledge will not be used inappropriately or as a weapon in a subsequent marital skirmish.

System: All relationships develop a predictable way of relating over time. This is done to preserve the equilibrium of the individuals in the relationship as well as to maintain balance, or homeostasis, in the relationship. So, in essence, a system is another type of defense. And the more rigid the system, the more people in it will strive to maintain the status quo, no matter how destructive it is. Perhaps the best adjective to describe a system is interlocking. That is, once a relationship has been ongoing for a period of time, the behavior and interactions of the individuals in that relationship become interdependent and are governed by implicit rules, as we saw in chapter 3. Therefore, rather than attribute a problem only to one person, people who think systemically believe that all participants in the system have a part in its creation and perpetuation. Systemic thinkers do not view the behavior of individuals in a vacuum; rather, they view individuals and their behavior as part of a broader context. This does not mean that individuals cannot change if the system does not support it, but it does mean that those who want to change should expect resistance. And the more rigid and dysfunctional the system, the greater the resistance they will experience. This is because the individuals in the system have a stake in perpetuating the status quo, no matter how dysfunctional. So changes should be undertaken cautiously and deliberately, as will be discussed in later chapters.

Symptoms: A symptom is the observable manifestation of a defense. Understanding the concept that symptoms can serve a function relies on grasping a basic paradox. Family systems therapists believe, because we have repeatedly witnessed this clinically, that as much as symptoms vex an individual or a family, they also accomplish something very important on another level as defenses. Further, this usually is outside people's awareness.

For example, if a family can distract itself by worrying about a specific problem, they are able to avoid enormous anxiety. This anxiety arises out of fears that the pain generated by the underlying problems of their intimate lives will be exposed and they will be left unprotected. In other words, symptoms serve a very important function in people's psychic economy and therefore, in reality, operate in their service. Even if the family and the symptomatic individual are paying a high price, unconsciously people feel that it is less than the one anticipated if their pain were exposed by dealing directly with their feelings. So both the system's cohesion and the individual's defenses are preserved by the symptom, even if the specific manifestation of the symptom appears to be tearing it apart.

While it may seem like one partner or the other is creating the problem with intimacy, usually both partners' contributions to their dynamics are intertwined. When relationships continue to operate in repetitive ways, then both people are getting something out of these destructive dynamics. Usually the payoff is protection from both having to be alone and genuinely together.

Complementarity: Because of our defenses, we all have the tendency to repeat what we know and to choose a partner who will help us play out our issues. We will be chosen by our partner to fulfill the same purpose. This, of course, allows the perpetuation of symptoms into the next generation. Often unwittingly, partners choose mates who will help them play out their unresolved loss, when the wise course would be to choose someone who will help them work it out. Smart and healthy people who initially may be attracted to these "stuck" individuals usually wise up and leave. Other stuck individuals may realize what they are doing to themselves and capitalize on the empathic connection that their partner or their therapist offers and resolve the loss once and for all. These relationships will genuinely last and contribute to both partners' growth, instead of continuing by virtue of inertia or because of the previous investment trap. But unless resolving the trauma and pain underlying the symptom does this, a direct assault on the defense or symptom likely will be met by resistance and opposition, and eventually the destruction of the relationship.

Defensive Styles of Partners with Unresolved Father Hunger

Unresolved father loss and the accompanying father hunger it creates ravage intimate relationships in myriad ways. What follows is a detailed discussion of the major relationship dynamics that are created when one or both partners experience unresolved father hunger. Although every relationship does not incubate each of the listed dynamics, upon close scrutiny, many of the following are found simultaneously. All of these dynamics make genuine intimacy difficult, if not impossible. This consciously may be seen as a bane, but unconsciously as a blessing. While unresolved father hunger interferes with the healthy development of relationships, at the same time, it becomes woven into their fabric.

Feeling Responses

Pervasive denial: Probably the single most important concept to keep in mind with people who have unresolved father loss is that they will likely have a high stake in keeping the loss where it has always been: out of sight and out of mind. So whatever the specific manifestation, the message is, "I don't want to feel what I truly feel." Hand-in-glove with that is the defensive tool that makes pervasive denial possible: "I don't even want to know what I feel!" This denial of emotions gradually becomes so pervasive that it eventually becomes a way of life. When this happens, people have colluded to create a mutual anesthetic. But this renders them incapable of solving their problems because of their need to deny the very existence of problems. In these instances, their problems and the symptoms that arise out of their inability to work effectively together to solve them clearly serve as effective distracters. Affairs, hiding behind children and substance abuse are common tools for denial.

Joe is a forty-one-year-old drug user who admits to using and selling drugs since he was thirteen. His father was a demanding, merciless and abusive critic of Joe. I theorized this was so the father didn't have to see his own inadequacies. Although Joe had literal scars from his father's physical mal-treatment of him, he freely confessed that the worst was his father's denigration of and disdain for him as a son. Whenever Joe and his wife became close, he became extremely afraid that his vulnerability would expose his inadequacies and weaknesses to her. So Joe orchestrated a fight as an excuse to smoke a joint. The cloud of smoke in which he lived allowed him to shroud his problems, to deaden his emotions and to keep his furious wife at a distance.

Ambivalent connections: As we saw in the last chapter, people who experienced poor or nonexistent relationships with their father are hungry for the affirmation, support and affection they did not get from him. They bring these needs—which can seem demanding because of their long-standing nature—into their relationships. This hunger can seem vora-cious and overpowering to their partner. Yet, presumably spouses share this wound and its accompanying neediness with their partner in the hope of getting salve, not to over-power the partner. However, because people usually pick a partner whose issues will hold up a mirror for them, it often is difficult for spouses to witness this wound because it triggers reverberations of their own hurt. Most people of either sex experience great difficulty in revealing their pain to one another, despite how much they may want to do so. And this is especially true for people with unresolved losses. So the "come here, go away" dance of intimacy these couples orchestrate usually comes from wanting to connect, to be seen and loved for who they really are, but not wanting to feel exposed and shamed because of what they want and need to reveal. This elaborate dance wards off the intimate overtures of their spouse while avoiding abandonment by not letting the spouse get too far away. Thus, people choose partners whose pathology resonates to the individuals' own damage, and a covert marital contract is struck that keeps both people's wounds sealed. This is the genesis of the ambivalence in relationships where unresolved loss, particularly one as significant as that of a father, looms in the background. And to compound the difficulty, these relationships often are imperiled in ways that usually are totally outside people's awareness, until it's too late.

Doris's father died ten years before she and Stan began treatment and three years before they were married. She was maddeningly inconsistent in her behavior and her emotions, and Stan was getting furious and fed up. Because I felt as though she did not really have both feet into the therapy, I speculated aloud that this perhaps was how she felt about her marriage as well. After much dancing around the issue, she finally confessed, "I don't commit to anything. When Stan and I got married, I never really committed to him. I decided I would never be that vulnerable again, after Dad died." She thought she had developed a foolproof way to protect herself from hurt and another abandonment—until she found out about Stan's affair.

Displaced anger: After sadness, anger is probably the second most common and natural emotional response to loss. And when a loss is felt in the acute phase, anger usually is evident at full volume and is directly related to the loss. Because anger is a natural response to abandonment, expressing it cleanly and clearly helps to resolve the loss. But when loss is chronic and unresolved, all emotions have long since gone underground. This, however, does not mean that they are no longer there. Usually, they leak out in the form of displaced anger that smolders just under the surface, waiting to explode at the slightest provocation. When the individual finally does express the anger, it usually is out of proportion to the situation, due to the freight that has been added. The angry person senses or believes that if anger were to be expressed directly rather than displaced, there would be a price to pay. So this anger often is expressed indirectly and inappropriately, especially among women for whom the expression of anger is culturally frowned upon, as we discussed in the last chapter. The biggest problem with displaced anger is that at the same time as it serves a protective, defensive function for the individual, it is diffuse and elusive. This makes it extremely difficult to identify the real source of the anger and to resolve it.

Mary, forty-eight, and Tom, fifty-one, have been married for twenty years. Most of that time, Tom has sought emotional connection and Mary has blocked it. The only girl and the youngest in a large and fiercely competitive group of siblings, Mary had an absent father and a hypercritical manic-depressive mother. So she grew up expecting to have to defend herself from attacks on all sides, which she did with the fervor and precision of a Green Beret. She's angry about: always feeling attacked, even when she's not; being left alone to take care of herself; feeling inept at protecting herself; always feeling wrong and wronged; and about her beloved first husband's serious mental illness that required that she take refuge in divorce. So when Tom approached her with a need, her automatic response was anger. Her anger was directed toward his mother for "ruining" him; his father for being ineffectual; him for having the need; and their adolescent daughter for mirroring Mary's struggles with identity development. But it really was at herself for her own perceived inadequacies.

Either flat or florid feelings: It is not human to lack feelings. Those who try to develop a Mr. Spock persona make themselves human robots. People handle emotions, those nasty reminders of their unresolved father hunger, in one of two ways, which are heads and tails of the same coin. In one case, they show no emotion. This flatness has become a defensive style adopted as a hedge against feeling anything, for fear that any emotions will result in the old, raw wound resurfacing. Or people exhibit a ubiquitous emotionality, usually displaced and misdirected, as Mary's was. This is an attempt to have feelings but to distract others from the real reason for the emotionality, which was the original wound. This is as a mother bird will fake an injury to lure a predator away from her baby. Many people think of the ability to express emotions as being synonymous with the ability to be intimate. And indeed, emotions are the prime legal tender in any relationship. Relationships where people cannot transact their emotions in an appropriate and satisfying way eventually become bankrupt. However, effusive emotionality often forms a block to genuine intimacy just as surely as showing no emotions does. It's hard to come close to a fire-breathing monster!

Tanya's parents divorced when she was six months old. After that, her mother remarried six more times, and she never saw her father again until her adolescence when she tried to go live with him. She reports that when she asked to do that, he said he did not want her, and her mother refused to give her permission anyway. So she was put in a foster home. At the age of forty she finally decided to make the commitment to marry. However, because of her difficulty in believing that anyone would stay, she orchestrated verbal brawls with Barry so that she could be the first to leave and to test him to see if he would stay. Then Barry disclosed to her his Internet affair, which was devastating "proof" to her that she never should have trusted. It took much longer for her to recognize her role in pushing him away from her and toward others.

Fear of expressing any feelings: As I have mentioned, partners with unresolved father hunger fear that an intimate partner's expression of emotion will resonate with one's own and thereby reopen the wounds of both. But they also subtly and perplexingly avoid even good feelings, for fear they will thaw denial because of the warmth associated with loving. The reasoning, however unconscious, goes something like, "If I let myself feel loving toward you, it will remind me of the love I have lost. And I can't do that without mourning, so I think I'll pass." This defensive strategy serves the dual purpose of containing emotions about both the current and the previous loved one.

Richard was adopted in infancy to a couple where the father was physically abusive and the mother ineffectual in stopping it. He spoke so softly that I could scarcely hear him as he told me his story. And his movements were so constricted as he sat across from me on the couch that I fantasized his apologizing for taking up so much air when breathing. Although he has experienced modest success as a health professional, he confessed to sabotaging himself. So he asked my help to find out why he undercut himself personally and professionally. After a session when he told me of his suddenly and defensively ending a three-year-long relationship with a woman he really loved, he called to cancel the next appointment and all future ones. And he wouldn't return my follow-up calls.

Feeling undeserving: People who don't feel worthy enough for their father to stay often develop calcified feelings of being generally undeserving. It is natural for children to blame themselves when deprived of a parent, particularly if it is a parent's choice and happens during an individual's egocentric years of childhood. This tendency often lingers into adulthood at an emotional level, even past the point where people can apply adult logic that can help them know better. This is because, by now, they have developed an entire personality style around feeling undeserving. So they act as if they are undeserving. The corollary to that is that very little good comes to them. While these people may engender empathy in others initially, unless their pitiful tune changes, others' responses soon turn to pity, and eventually these hapless people succeed in getting themselves abandoned again. Thus, they can have another layer of "proof" of their unworthiness. These people make good victims.

Jerry's father died of cancer when Jerry was ten years old. When his mother informed the child of his father's death, her words as he remembered them were, "Jerry, you don't have a father." Using a child's magical thinking, he decided that

meant that he didn't deserve to have a father, either. When he
showed up for marital therapy twenty years later, he had been
fired from his job and his new bride was at her wit's end and
threatening divorce because she could not understand why he
would not let her love him. He finally succeeded in convincing her that he was unworthy of her love, so she initiated "the
divorce from hell." This was the proof he needed to convince
himself he could do nothing right.

Feeling shame: In addition to the shame I discussed in the
last chapter that comes from the wound of father hunger,
people often feel shame for needing to keep hidden something
so   significant and yet so painful. Sometimes they even
develop shame for loving and caring in the first place. Or they
feel ashamed that their love was so puny that they were unable
to get their father's attention. Whether it is necessary or not,
people commonly develop shame when they believe they have
something to hide, even if what they must hide is something
natural like grief in the face of a loss. Therefore, what starts
out as a normal set of feelings mushrooms into a family secret
that becomes humiliating because it must be kept hidden.
When the message is that family members must keep a loss
to themselves, the whole family becomes enmeshed in a
conspiracy of silence.

Bobby was the only son of a highly intellectual father and a
traditional housewife mother. During most of Bobby's childhood, his father was working toward a Ph.D. in an erudite and
esoteric field. Bobby remembers few father-son interactions
and even fewer times when the two played together. One particular time he does remember is when his father took him

fishing, but his father sat by himself reading a book the whole time. So Bobby concluded that his father saw himself merely as transportation and that he didn't enjoy being with his son anyway. When Bobby shared this in session, his sobs came from so deep that he wailed in pain. The most hurtful part of this experience and myriad others like it were how helpless they made Bobby feel about either getting his father's attention or deserving his love. And worse yet, it made him feel ashamed of his own ability to love. From that, he concluded that his love and his capacity to show it meant nothing. This, of course, made him an ideal candidate to partner with a woman who expected abandonment.

Behavioral Responses

By now, it is abundantly clear that a major motivation among those who have experienced a previous loss, even if it is resolved, is to avoid getting hurt again. And the fear repeating the hurt is usually even greater for those who have experienced an unresolved loss that they continue to deny. Many of these people believe, on some irrational and unconscious level, that they would not survive another loss. So they display predictable behaviors designed to help them avoid both losing again and facing the previous loss.

In addition to the affective manifestations of this fear discussed earlier, there are numerous behavioral expressions of an unresolved loss. Although these same behaviors may be rooted in a cause other than a loss, clinically when I see these behavioral indicators as well as the emotional responses listed earlier, I begin my detective work to tease out whether or not father loss is at the heart of the problem.

Difficulty making commitments: People who have experienced unresolved loss are usually highly conflicted about intimacy. They want a commitment because being alone is so terrifying, but they shy away from it because they fear losing again. So most avoid commitment and remain detached in relationships so they can bail out easily and first. Men are particularly susceptible to this because of their socialization emphasizing autonomy. Their struggle typically is learning how to face their partner and protect themselves from her at the same time. Still other men feel that a commitment will limit their freedom, cramp their style and demand too much of them. Yet, at the same time, most want to belong. Therefore, they experience what psychologist Samuel Osherson called the "attachment battle."[5] This is the inner conflict between their need to connect and their reluctance to do so.

While commitment phobia may have formerly been primarily the province of men, more and more young women whose parents divorce often have difficulty with commitment as well. Too many attempt to remain detached and uncommitted as a self-protective measure. This was a major finding of psychologist Judith Wallerstein's ten-year follow-up study of children of divorce. She labeled this phenomenon "the sleeper effect."[6] She found that girls who suffered no apparent ill effects at the time of their parents' divorce become preoccupied with an intolerable level of anxiety about betrayal when it was age-appropriate to commit to a relationship themselves. They often believe that commitment is impossible, and they experience intense jealousy verging on obsession. These women are deeply worried about relationships. They want to believe in commitment and love. They want to marry and have children. They want to do it "right" the first time. But they are tremendously afraid that they can't and won't. These women, who seemed well adjusted in childhood and adolescence, especially when compared to their brothers, move into the passage to adulthood that involves commitment to a relationship. Then, "wham! They encounter the sleeper effect."[7] Fear of betrayal overwhelms the lives of too many children of divorce, as was in the case of Barbara.

Barbara was a beautiful young woman who had just graduated with honors from a prestigious private Midwestern college. When Barbara sat across from me our first session, I was struck by the contrast between the deliberateness of her speech and the impulsiveness of her actions. Recently engaged, she reported that whenever Tim mentioned setting a wedding date, she impulsively had sex with one of his friends—it didn't matter to her which one. As I probed for factors that would help Barbara make sense of her puzzling and precarious behavior, she shared that her parents had divorced when she was fourteen years old when both began affairs with another couple who were friends. Barbara was the apple of her father's eye, and after the separation, he said that he moved fifteen minutes away supposedly so that his children would have easy access to him. Yet, he seldom came around, even for scheduled visitations. His career, new relationship and blaming his wife for both affairs took precedence. Barbara felt crushed and shunted aside, both by the divorce and by her father's lack of consistent attention. So she found a way with Tim to get her mind playing tricks on herself that she could protect herself from the risk of trusting again by being untrustworthy first.

Passive-aggressive style: When people develop a passive-aggressive style, they do so to mask smoldering anger. Then, their anger is not directed where it belongs. In fact, it is not directed at all. This is because these people know, however unconsciously, that they can ill afford to sit down and figure out what really is the matter. This kind of introspection and communication just might lead them back to the loss they have been trying to ignore or that long ago passed into their unconscious. These people do a slow burn and act out subtly but maddeningly instead. These people are usually downright manipulative. That is, they manipulate others to get their way; and they manipulate themselves in order to stay out of their own emotional mischief.

Louise and Charlie's perennial marital fight was about money: who spent it, who deserved more of it and on what it was spent. They had fought so long, hard and unsuccessfully about this that after they had exhausted themselves one too many times, they agreed to begin marital therapy. After one particularly frustrating session, Louise went to a local department store, charged three thousand dollars worth of goods for herself and for their home, and "forgot" to tell her husband, until the bill arrived.

Expecting partner to deny emotions and problems: Because of the degree of denial of people with unresolved loss, they unconsciously expect that their partner will deny in kind. Most wish to keep the loss where it has always been: out of sight and out of mind. If the loss predates the marriage as most we are considering here do, the partner often is chosen with that expectation in mind. Otherwise, their covers would be blown. And woe to a spouse in this kind of relationship who stumbles into expressing emotions or who seeks to solve relationship problems! People know intuitively that vulnerability and the resulting intimacy can thaw their denial, so they avoid it. It is as if they say, "If I let myself feel deeply toward you and even need you, it will remind me of the love I have lost and of how afraid I am of losing again. So go away and let me keep my distance! But don't go too far away because I can't handle loss." For those who refuse to accede to the covert contract that their partner attempts to extract, the sanctions they receive are usually swift and can be severe. Just how harsh depends on the degree of rigidity of the person who needs to deny and the pathology in the relationship system they together have created. Unless both partners collude, however, these relationships do not survive. Those relationships governed by the contract to collude to maintain distance too often continue but cut everyone in the family to emotional ribbons by the unrelenting conflict or by its members leading totally separate lives.

Tara was a thirty-eight-year-old woman who had been married to Sam for twenty-one years. For years, she begged her husband to change, blaming him for their problems, waiting impotently for him to change. When they finally began family therapy, she and her adolescent daughter were in constant verbal brawls so that she was not required to examine herself, her own contributions to their family's mess or to learn to deal directly with Sam. Her family's Cinderella, she was oldest of eight children, all very close in age. Slowly, she began to discover how she, too, had blocked communication in her marriage, even though she always blamed Sam for this. She said with profuse tears:

If I shared my loneliness and it took him back to his, I couldn't handle it. I want him to do that, but something in me says that I want him to be strong, too. So there's this push/pull in me. I guess I can see what you've been saying, that I get in the way of his working on his stuff. Earlier in the week when he was sharing more, it was great. But then I started having trouble [with it]. So I shut him down.

For people conflicted about intimacy, the Chinese proverb "Be careful what you wish for" clearly applies.

Denies needs: When a partner becomes overtly needy and is willing to take responsibility for those needs, the other partner doesn't have to guess or to mind read. Owning needs and taking responsibility to ask that they be met gives each partner a fair chance of opting to meet those needs. However, as we have said, more often than not, people who are chronically grieved prefer to keep their vulnerability hidden, especially from themselves, lest they become overwhelmed and feel shamed by it. But hiding, of course, does not make the vulnerability or the loss go away. It usually just resurfaces in another form. Emotionally connecting with a partner often generates anxiety that comes of getting closer. So for many, it just seems easier not to connect in the first place. In order not to be intimate, however, they must deny their needs. Strategies that people use to deny their needs typically are: food abuse as an attempt to control or fill their hunger, or to assuage it by the attention that alarmed family members give; anger run amock as an attempt to cauterize hurt and vulnerability; the inability to make relationships work because of an unwillingness to risk and to invest; or overinvolvement with children because relating to them is not threatening as it is with partners and peers.

Jonathan was a highly eligible bachelor in his mid-thirties when he began therapy. Although he had fancied himself a "ladies' man" since high school, he had truly loved only once, and that woman summarily dumped him (I surmised, because of his arrogance). Despite the fact that this relationship had ended years ago, Jon was still clueless about why. So he requested my help in figuring out why he seemed unable to relate to women in a satisfying way. I began an early session as I customarily do by asking what he needed to work with that day. The response he shot back was, "Need to? Nothing! I don't need to work on anything. I'll survive without it. But I might want to work on the ski trip I'm going on with some friends next week."

Difficulty with separation and individuation: One main reason that people grow into strong and separate individuals is because they have had secure and clear attachments to their primary caregivers in childhood. When individuals have experienced a healthy separation process from their parents, they in turn can foster it with their own children and tolerate it with their spouse. But when they have not, their ability to participate in healthy relationships where both autonomy and togetherness are valued and possible will be compromised. Thus, true independence paradoxically first requires dependence. In fact, the man widely acknowledged to be the grandfather of family therapy, Nathan Ackerman, believes that the only true autonomy is in togetherness.[8] To that I add that the only true togetherness is in autonomy. That is, people who first are genuinely strong and healthy individuals make the most satisfying connections in relationships. And I further believe that, rather than being totally self-focused as some in the human potential movement would prefer for us, *the best opportunity to learn who one is and to develop one's individuality comes in the context of relationships of all kinds.*

Scott was the managing partner of a small law firm and the father of four children. He was overinvolved with his daughter and disinterested in his sons. He had grown up a lonely, only child of parents who instrumentally took care of him but with whom he felt no emotional connection. In one of my many attempts to help him see the significance of his father's emotional absence from his life, I suggested that he see the movie *Field of Dreams*. He came to the next session totally puzzled about why so many men in the theater cried during a movie about baseball. Clearly, we had more work to do! After many months, when I thought he finally could identify with the subject of father loss and claim his disowned needs, I suggested that he rent the movie and watch it again. This released a torrent of pent-up tears and precipitated a spontaneous late-night visit with his father. He literally cried on his father's shoulder and told him how much he loved and needed him.

Then Scott proudly opened the session following his visit with his father announcing, "I've joined the club of men!" He then went on to describe how, now that he had confessed his needs and gotten them met, he finally could imagine surviving his eighty-year-old father's death. Now that he finally had a relationship with his father, paradoxically, he could afford to let it go. He volunteered, "I used to think that if he were to die,

I couldn't go on living because we weren't separate. He was me. Now I'll be sad. And I'll miss him terribly. But I'll be all right."

Fearing loss of control: A common response of spouses where unresolved loss fuels their marital dynamics is that one or the other is controlling. The unconscious aim is to stop or at least to manipulate interactions that could lead to the expression of emotions, generate vulnerability and create close feelings. Although often this blocking may appear to be done for loving reasons ("Cheer up! It's not so bad!"), most often in reality it is self-protective. Maybe this behavior is as subtle as not listening as partners reminisce. Or maybe it is as blatant as calling partners weak and telling them to stop living in the past. In still other instances, controlling people try to get their partner's attention back by injunctions like, "Stop feeling sorry for yourself!" Some people even become symptomatic themselves to distract the partner from grieving. The bottom line in understanding controlling people who rely on power plays is grasping the basic paradox of how powerless they feel.

Lucinda and Dan came to marital therapy ostensibly because of sexual dysfunction. However, in the first session, Lucinda made two significant disclosures. One was that she was sick and tired of being Dan's caretaker. Dan had been depressed, seeing psychiatrists and on medication for their entire eighteen-year marriage. She also confessed that she secretly suspected that her disinterest in sex, or in any closeness with Dan for that matter, might have something to do with her father's death when she was eighteen years old and her fear of being abandoned again. After months of clearing a path so that Lucinda finally could grieve for her father, Dan became visibly and by his own admission more depressed. Lucinda said during the next session that maybe she should stop this grief work if it were going to upset Dan, even though she thought she was finally getting somewhere. At this Dan noticeably grinned. To make it both safe and possible to get back to work on resolving her grief, we first needed to relieve Dan of the need to control her process, their relationship and our therapy by once again becoming symptomatic. Only then could she emotionally bury her father.

Competitiveness: There are many reasons that people are competitive. One is that they are trying to prove their worth. Another is so they can tell themselves they will never be controlled by others or by their need for them. Still another is trying to finally win the approval of someone whose attention or favor they never got. Underneath it all is the attempt to block feelings and vulnerability. But most competitive people, when they are being honest, recognize the tremendous toll that being competitive takes on themselves and on their relationships.

Martin was a thirty-five-year-old former football and wrestling star in both high school and college. True to everyone's expectations, he began to ascend the corporate ladder almost immediately on being hired. However, when he began to examine the role that our culture's expectation that men be competitive had in his misery with his wife, he said the following: "It's tremendously overwhelming to always have to put the mark higher on the wall. There's never a sense of completion or satisfaction. There's always more, better stuff, higher, faster stuff. As males, we skip that class, that part of life that gets us in touch with our feelings."

Summary

What is the sum total of all these factors? What kinds of relationships do people with chronic, unresolved father loss create?

- Their relationships are often based on convenience and coexistence rather than intimacy, because emotional closeness could be threatening or too close for comfort.

- Partners often collude with each other to keep their loss or losses out of sight and out of mind.

- Partners in these relationships easily become polarized. One kind of polarization typically is that they become either extremely enmeshed (where one person does the thinking and feeling for both, and both are highly consensus-sensitive) or extremely disengaged (where couples live like room-mates or in a business arrangement without any obvious emotional connection). Another typical kind of polarization is that one person is the worker bee and the other expects to be taken care of as the queen or king bee. Still another kind of polarization is the open conflict of refusing to agree on anything, including what day it is.

- Partners' sexual relationship often is strained or nonexistent because of the need to keep a distance.

- Anger is frequently used to distance so no one feels threatened by too much closeness and to connect so people can kiss and make up.

- Power struggles are common.

- Unexpressed mutual neediness or the inability to negotiate meeting one's own and each other's needs makes both partners emotional children.

- For these dynamics to persist, both partners must collude to keep them going. If one partner refuses to keep playing the game of hide-and-seek, it cannot continue. Although this choice may end the relationship eventually, aware partners must decide how much sacrificing they are willing to do in the service of the relationship. It is hoped that this decision is made before there are children involved, so that the legacy of loss does not come down the generations to them.

Loss, even one in the acute phase, has the extraordinary capability of negatively impacting relationships. Paradoxically, the loss of someone as significant as a father, who has long ago passed into the unconscious, generates even more suffering in its wake. This is because, as David Viscott says, "Avoiding pain is the beginning of suffering."[9] It is important that mental health professionals and laypeople alike understand this so that those relationships that are viable can be insulated and healed, and so that those that need to end can do so in ways that don't generate another round of unresolved losses for all involved.

People who have experienced chronic, unresolved loss, especially one as powerful as the loss of a parent, have learned many coping skills that have helped them keep loss out of sight and out of mind. And they will need to unlearn those skills so they will no longer need their protective Plexiglas shield and can learn more healthy, functional ways of being. While some are resourceful enough to accomplish both the deconstruction and the reconstruction processes on their own, many will require professional help. When to go for help, how to help loved ones who are chronically grieved and how to help oneself will be discussed in subsequent chapters.

References

1. David Viscott, *Emotional Resilience: Simple Truths for Dealing with the Unfinished Business of Your Past* (New York: Random House Audiobooks, 1996).

2. Robert Ackerman, *Perfect Daughters: Adult Children of Alcoholics* (Deerfield Beach, Fla.: Health Communications, 1989), 25.

3. Ibid., 35.

4. Mavis Hetherington, "How Do We Define the Best Interests of the Child?" (paper presented at the Continuing Education Conference of the American Psychological Association and the American Bar Association, Los Angeles, 1997).

5. Samuel Osherson, *Wrestling with Love: How Men Struggle with Intimacy* (New York: Fawcett Columbine, 1992), 4.

6. Judith Wallerstein and Sandra Blakeslee, *Second Chances: Men, Women and Children a Decade After Divorce* (New York: Ticknor & Fields, 1989), 63.

7. Ibid.

8. Nathan Ackerman, *The Psychodynamics of Family Life* (New York: Basic Books, 1958), 15.

9. Viscott, *Emotional Resilience: Simple Truths for Dealing with the Unfinished Business of Your Past.*

7

Spiritual Issues and Father Loss

*In the midst of winter,
I finally learned that there was in
me an invincible summer.*

—Albert Camus
Actuelles

Pain doesn't travel in straight lines; it circles around behind us. Why, in the midst of a loss, which is hard enough to cope with, do we often run smack into a spiritual crisis that further compounds our angst? Out of the depths we cry out for help, only to feel that none is available. Instead of an answer to our demands to know why or why me, all we hear is resounding silence. The challenge at those times is to stay in the struggle that is this dark night of the soul. The rewards are genuine comfort, transcendent meaning and a sense that life is unspeakably precious. Instead, all too often, people throw up their hands in despair, and anomie and alienation replace the peace they could have.

As Caroline Myss said, "You can only move with God as mature as you are."[1] People's concepts of a higher power can be affected by their underlying psychological state and level of maturity. In desperation, they may construct a higher power to rescue them as their own personal *deus ex machina*, and then feel cheated and resentful when that appears to fail. Others act as if they believe that they have a hotline to heaven that gets them the definitive answer regarding the Lord's will. Still others don't dare, or don't know how to ask, and see little reason to believe their petitions will be heard anyway. In prosperous times, people tend to ignore the idea of divine intervention completely, instead crediting themselves for their good fortune. But when something goes wrong, it is easy, even automatic, to blame God. Thus, it is not surprising that father loss, because it has so many subtle and specific dimensions, can raise unique spiritual issues. It did for me.

As I am writing *Longing for Dad* I feel overwhelmed at the enormity of the task presented by this chapter. I know it's because I am trying to be too academic and defensive about an immensely personal and emotional subject. It is difficult to expose myself and my old wounds even to myself. I would just as soon leave intact the scars that have formed over those deep wounds, rather than rubbing them raw by this chapter. I want to turn away, distracting myself with this mundane task or that. I stumble over words. My mind goes blank. I have trouble collecting my thoughts. Mostly, I want to run from them. I fret that I simply am not up to the task. I feel alone and depressed. I surprise myself by crying old tears out of the depths of my soul.

People who experience a spiritual crisis catalyzed by having to deal with father loss usually cope by going in one of several directions. One is to develop a grudge against God, which seeds the fertile ground of belief in nothing and nobody. Another, in attempting to master the risks inherent in trusting, people will sometimes develop the childlike faith of the religious fundamentalist. Thus, they create a simplistic deity to replace their lost father. Yet another is to deny there is a God or any rationality to the universe because of the absence of proof. Still another is to search for meaning that both is required for and comes from developing a mature and transcendent faith. Once the trauma is appropriately resolved, people do not need a make-believe God, but can look to their higher power as a strong presence in their life. I acknowledge that some people believe that any concept of God is an imaginary construct. However, those people are deprived of a very powerful source of comfort for dealing with loss.

In most religious traditions, we drape our concept of God in a paternal and paternalistic cloak. The Godhead is male and a father figure. Therefore, people who feel abandoned by their earthly father will likely have great difficulty trusting that a heavenly father will not leave them, too. If both their earthly father and heavenly father abandon them, people's responses usually fit into one of two broad categories. Some oppose and reject all authority. They find no succor in a concept of God at all and likely will become agnostics. Others who hungrily long for a father will search out anything and anyone who will fit that bill. They are the most susceptible to the lure of a cult or of a fundamentalist's pat answers.

With the benefit of twenty/twenty hindsight, I can now see several explanations for why my pain from my own father loss cut extra deep. The main reason was my perception about my situation. I see now that in attempting to cope with my own father loss, I was thinking with remnants of a childlike fundamentalist faith and my adult, educated views of religion. Both were simplistic ways of thinking. Neither was sufficient or helped me to find peace. In fact, they only intensified my problem:

> My dad's death and my "reburial" of him that was catalyzed by my first sister's death were part of a chain reaction of losses for me. All told, by the time it was done, I had experienced four deaths of immediate family members in four and a half years. Three of the four died suddenly, giving no forewarning and the accompanying preparation time. The only death where shock didn't add to the trauma was Mother's, which was slow and agonizing. Because her first cancer was diagnosed only four months after Dorothy died, and it took eight cancers to kill my stoic mother, the specter of her death formed a macabre back-drop for each of the subsequent deaths. This also meant that she had to go through a second child's funeral with lips so blistered from chemotherapy that it hurt to cry. But this time, her stoicism gave way as she literally was unable to avoid crying. So once again, I was forced to hear my mother's anguished cries. Only this time, I was mad!

I began to be steeped in a religious tradition when I started Sunday school at the age of three. Because I had been taught as a child that God was omnipotent, I expected him to do something to take away my pain and to do it virtually on demand. Intellectually, I could accept that death is a part of life and that we all have to go sometime—but why so much at once? And for that matter, where was God when this happened in the first place? Why hadn't he intervened to protect us from this agony that went beyond the pale? Surely it was more than a family, particularly one as devout as ours, could bear or even should have to! When my Jewish therapist referred to this chain reaction of tragedy as a holocaust for me, I finally felt that my emotional reaction was understandable and even warranted.

Another reason I felt so desperately alone was that if my beloved Daddy had abandoned me, why would God be any different? All I could hear from both of these fathers was silence. Even as a teenager when I was sent to our church's leadership school, I earnestly wished and prayed for a sense of God's presence, and once again, all I got back was resounding silence. I did not know at the time that I had linked earthly and heavenly fathers. Because my dad, the father I loved and trusted more than any other human being, couldn't be relied upon to stay, why would my heavenly father be any different?

When Mother finally died, I was psychically on my knees. I was angry, wounded, bereft and again felt totally abandoned by everyone, including and especially God. I cried out, and all I heard was a resounding silence. Would I ever be able to come to terms with it all? Where was God? If this were what God's help was like, no thanks; I'd go it alone! Surely it couldn't get any worse than this! I bellowed at God like a gored bull. I shook my fists at the heavens. I felt totally forsaken. The cascade of questions I couldn't answer never left my tear-stained head. What had we done to have to lose Mother now, too, when we were still walking wounded from the others? Hadn't we suffered enough? I demanded to know the inscrutable from God. Slowly and gradually, I began to find answers.

What helped were simple things. Living in Chicago at the time, I took long, solitary walks along the shores of Lake

Michigan winter and summer. And I would force myself to sit in my rocking chair trying to center, in hopes of regaining a semblance of equilibrium that had been so toppled by these crises. My resistance to facing myself was strong; first I'd check my answering machine, then I'd return calls, then I'd remember to add an item to my to-do list, then I'd check my mail. You know the drill. But when I could finally settle myself down, I pondered and listened.

Slowly, it began to dawn on me that I needed to learn to listen and to discern, not demand or even ask. So I would make tea and sit for hours, rocking, pondering and looking out the window at the huge oak tree whose changing colors promised that life indeed would go on. I needed to empty my head of the clatter so I could hear answers in the silence. And I needed to cry; there was always a pile of tissues when I finished.

I also searched out a community. Being single at the time, this was essential. Grieving is a lonely enough process. Yet, "This solitary work we cannot do alone."[2] After much seeking, I finally found a church that fit for me because of a handful of kindred spirits. Even though it was not the denomination in which I had been reared, it was more important to me that I find a communion of saints than a particular doctrine. I was accepted into the choir, and we sang glorious music! Mendelssohn's *Elijah*, Handel's *Messiah*, Faure's *Requiem* and Bach's *Magnificat*. Because music had been my first way of communicating, singing brought me back to my roots and my home in very important, direct and soothing ways. Because of that, sometimes I was unable to sing for the lump in my throat and the tears in my eyes. But music hath powers to soothe the savage breast, so I kept trying, at two rehearsals a week and two services every Sunday morning. In that choir, I met a woman who became and has remained one of my best friends, even though fifteen years and fifteen hundred miles have intervened. I had found a place I could belong for a while in a city that I loved. I think of Chicago as my second home, an oasis when everything felt foreign and askew from the platelets of my life shifting higgledy-piggledy underneath me.

During the worst of my agony, I requested a meeting with our pastor, to which he readily agreed. He knew of my situation from my friends, and he had been waiting for the opportunity to help. As I sat down uneasily in his easy chair, I began the litany of all that had happened. I also confessed how enraged I was at God. I wasn't sure whether I would be struck by lightning for daring to voice this secret, but I figured I had little to lose by that point. If God truly were a vengeful God and I would be punished for my temerity, surely no punishment could be worse than this! Instead of condemnation or even pity, the pastor simply said he understood. He invited me to vent everything, and vent I did! I wailed and I railed until my fury was spent. Then he simply asked: Would I pray with him? He said a quiet prayer. And that was all. I have no idea what he said, but I know that when I left his office, I was done being angry.

It was nearly Lent. In our area, a group of churches marked Good Friday by a daylong service of music, homilies and silent reflection centered around the seven last words of Christ. A deeply concerned friend went with me, and we watched and prayed. I listened, and finally I heard. "Let this cup pass from me. Nevertheless, not my will but Thy will."

Finally, I understood that I had no control. All I could do—and needed to do—was accept. If God could not even spare Jesus, his beloved son, it was arrogant of me to expect that I should be spared! But God could be with me if I would accept it. Mendelssohn's song that our choir had sung, that I couldn't get through with dry eyes, finally made sense: "Cast thy burdens upon the Lord and He will sustain thee." I finally got it. We can't expect that God will rescue us; but we can allow God to be with us. While our glorious music ministered to the congregation, we were ministering to me as well.

I know now that I heard God's silence because that is what I heard, not because he was silent. I just didn't know how to feel his presence or where to look for it. Because of this, it took me a while to learn to experience my sister Dorothy's ongoing presence, which I finally came to feel when the sun came in through the window in a certain way or when a gentle breeze brushed my cheek. However, until I developed this way of knowing, I again compounded my own agony by what amounted to a difficulty trusting. This issue, of course, played out and recycled over and over in my adult intimate relationships with men.

Bottom line: I simply didn't understand that aloneness is part of the human condition, and that no one and nothing can make that go away. And even when I began to grasp this, I didn't want to accept it. But finally, I understood that we all must die alone, just as we must endure galvanizing experiences in life alone, because they are ours. Caring people can go with us as far as they can to help us manage painful experiences, but only we can do the doing. And the sooner we accept this, the better. Then we can quit fighting our higher power and ourselves. Not even God is powerful enough to take away painful experiences from us. But the rainbow he offers is to be with us. And if we are open to it, others can be with us as well. But they can only accompany us, they cannot face the pain for us.

I have learned many important truths from that harrowing time in my life. Among them: to value the small things; that my life is precious; that people who understand are worth their weight in gold and are God made manifest; that life is worth living, regardless; not to fear death, even if dying of a dreaded disease is harrowing. And I've learned that God is with me, as are my loved ones who have gone before. I have endured agony that truly goes beyond the pale and have come out the other side as strong as tempered steel. And although I wouldn't wish what I endured on my worst enemy, I wouldn't trade it for the world. It has made me who I am.

The only thing I would do differently is to get a kitten. They are pure and unadulterated comfort as they snuggle in and purr, as our Rudy did, apparently sensing my distress as I wrote this.

Trauma and Transformation

The nature of trauma of all kinds is captured by the Chinese character for the word *crisis—wei gei*. This character is actually two symbols superimposed on one another, one representing danger, and the other opportunity.[3] People in crisis stand at a crossroads. If they handle the crisis appropriately, it can provide grist for what in the end will be a growth-producing and ego-strengthening journey. This is the case, even when people think they are going to die of pain if they face themselves and the crisis at hand, and even sometimes wish they would! Transformation happens because of and despite the pain involved in the process. In the end, genuine healing for most people comes not just from paying attention to the psychological issues and practical concerns involved in a loss. It comes from attention to the spiritual dimensions inherent in the trauma as well.

However, the spirits of all too many are broken when their hearts are broken by trauma. Then, they are never the same again, unless they get therapeutic and spiritual help. When they do not, the whole of their development eventually becomes arrested in their failed attempts to put the past in the past and move on. What these people apparently do not realize is that *it is not what happens to people that is important; rather, it is how they handle what happens to them that makes the difference.* People's management of and adaptation to a trauma will govern whether their crisis represents danger or offers a unique opportunity for fundamental and substantive change. Trauma truly changes people's life, for better or for worse.

Often at the beginning of treatment, clients have not yet grasped what they must do to change their lives and not just their behavior. All they know is that they are miserable. So they send competing messages. In essence, they imply, "I'm miserable! Help me change. But don't change a thing. And tell me something I can do that I don't have to do and that won't change me." Obviously, meeting all of these covert demands is impossible because one contradicts the other. Nor is attempting to do so wise because that allows, and even encourages, people to stay stuck. Only when people are courageous enough to tackle the issues underlying and, therefore, fueling their unhappiness will they, as the popular slogan goes, "get a life."

A Critical Distinction

Spiritual crisis generated by father loss is not for the religious only. People do not need to subscribe to the tenets of a particular religion to have spiritual questions or to need to resolve them in order to be in and transformed by a crisis. In some ways, it may be easier for those who do not subscribe to a particular religion to come to terms because, as I experienced, the remnants of my childlike views of God clearly were partially the cause of my spiritual conundrum. The issues for all who struggle with such a profound loss do not pertain to doctrine and dogma, as does religion. While sometimes practicing a particular form of religion may be comforting and facilitative to people's bereavement process, all too often, platitudes like "It was God's will" and rigid religious beliefs only deepen the crisis. How can a loving God have wanted a horrible loss to happen?

Instead, spiritual matters are transcendent and, at their base, are of the heart and soul. They are based in the search for meaning that Viktor Frankl described in his classic work about his experiences in Nazi camps.[4] That is, to resolve a loss, people must both discern a meaning for the trauma itself and redefine their life and find meaning for it now, even in the face of the loss. These philosophical, existential issues are independent of specific religious practices or dogma.

Because of the psychological implications and the urgency of finding satisfactory spiritual resolution to the pain of father loss, I write this book and as a psychologist have the temerity to include this chapter. Even though I am not a member of the clergy, I strongly believe that grappling with spiritual issues is essential to postloss recovery, regardless of the nature or the circumstances of the loss. Moreover, because spiritual issues are at the core of what defines and creates people's humanness, they are never the sole provinces of the religious.

Spiritual Issues That Often
Accompany Father Loss

Aloneness is at the core of the existential human dilemma. Fear of being alone and being unloved and unlovable are the basis of why human beings are relational. These fears are also what propel some people into unhealthy relationships so that they neither have to be alone nor grieve their father loss. Perhaps hoping for the promise that they never have to be alone is why people search for comfort in the spiritual realm. Because the fear of being alone is endemic to the human condition even in the best of times, this fear can take on a life of its own and become overpowering in the November of the soul. Aloneness is frequently a major reason why people shut down and do not resolve the loss at the time it occurs.

Facing a loss is difficult enough when people have adequate social supports. But when they feel they have to go through it alone, the isolation itself can be devastating. Many defend against the abject pain of suffering in silence by walling it and themselves off. Sending it underground only forces us to carry the pain with us, however unconsciously. Then, all too often, to block their pain, people build a psychic barricade around themselves. No one can penetrate to hurt them; but they are trapped and cannot easily come out. This defensive maneuver backfires because it virtually ensures that people remain isolated, even if they have found someone who will spend time with them. This frequently results in two more crises loading onto the original trauma. Defending against the need to face the trauma is itself a problem. Then, this denial of the problem often triggers crises in both the relational and spiritual realms.

In the face of a loss, it is easy and natural to feel over-whelmed and small, virtually swallowed up in the crisis that seems to conspire to make mourners feel even more isolated. When my sister died, I was incensed that the rest of the world was going on and leaving me behind to grieve. It felt like my life had stopped when hers was snuffed out. It is normal to feel diminished and impotent in the face of trauma. When my mother was dying of cancer, one of my greatest pains was being unable to heal her. Both the painful experience and the spiritual crisis it can generate have the potential to cause people to feel insignificant and inept, as they go "Alone into the Alone," as C. S. Lewis wrote in his classic work about facing the death of a loved one.[5] However, for most, the agony that is an essential part of grief is muted only by the sense of community to help make it through the dark time. Love not only begets love—it transmits strengths if we let people in.

People who grieve perhaps face the greatest challenge of their lives. Those who rise to the challenge are forever trans-formed by it. Many times spiritual questions go unanswered because the challenge is so daunting. It was certainly tempt-ing for me to try this tack. However, resolving the spiritual crisis resolves the trauma at the same time because the final step in resolving a loss relates to redefining one's life in light of the loss while incorporating the meaning of it into one's future life. That is how central this philosophical struggle is to the resolution of the loss and moving on.

Yet, our society's typical attitude toward pain is to take a pill and wait for it to go away. People then feel confused, anxious, and helpless when that does not work and their strong and painful emotions persist. These people must real-ize that getting over a loss requires three simple elements: talk about it; cry about it; and sit with it. Resist the temptation to change the subject; otherwise, the relief from the pain will be transitory and problematic.

Core Spiritual Issues Inherent in Father Loss

Both from my personal experiences with loss and from my work as a therapist, time and again I have observed that there are some special spiritual risks from father loss that deserve highlighting because they are central to the spiritual crisis that generally accompanies a loss. I do not offer this as a final or complete list, and readers are encouraged to add their own ideas. However, my experience suggests that these are givens for most people willing to contemplate the spiritual dimension.

Discerning readers also will note the absence of answers here. This is deliberate. It is the height of disrespect to imply that there are pat answers to huge existential questions, that there is one answer or that one has the answer to someone else's conundrum. It is even more disrespectful to imply that one knows how others should lead their lives. That is for each of us to discern and to decide. Conversely, it is highly healing to people to help them frame their own questions and then to be with them, literally and emotionally, as they struggle to answer them.

Feeling Deserving of Bad or Undeserving of Good

Probably the first question people ask themselves in the wake of a trauma is the anguished cry of Job in the Old Testament: "Why me, O Lord?" This issue can be a real stickler, especially for people who grew up in a religious tradition that emphasized original sin; an eye for an eye and a tooth for a tooth, punishment for transgressions; and salvation by good works. Often, these beliefs are deeply ingrained. In these sorts of traditions, it seems logical and right to blame oneself. If people's model for spirituality is one where humans are puppets controlled by an angry or punitive father-figure God whom they must please or be damned, two logical conclusions often are reached simultaneously. When something bad happens, people must not have deserved what is good from their father and must have deserved what is bad from him. In an effort to help people come to grips with how they are unnecessarily tortured by these beliefs as well as to understand his own son's rare and terminal medical condition, Rabbi Harold Kushner wrote the bestseller *When Bad Things Happen to Good People*. I recommend this to readers who need further guidance in examining their problematic beliefs on this issue.

Jack was in his mid-thirties when he finally acceded to his wife's demand that they begin marital therapy or else. He was the youngest of six brothers who each had learned to attack the underdog from their extremely abusive father. It was not the physical abuse that was so bad; it was the mental and emotional abuse that tortured Jack even into adulthood. By his explicit and implicit messages, the father literally and figuratively pounded it into Jack's head that the boy was worthless. He taught his sons to steal, and would berate them if the cache they brought back wasn't big and impressive enough. Once, as a teenager, Jack did a jewelry heist worth a quarter of a million dollars, hoping that maybe this would garner his father's praise. Instead, when Jack brought it home, the father went on a rampage because he hadn't bagged more, so Jack defiantly broke in again and took it back.

Although he never got caught, he of course lived in fear that he would. These robberies themselves could easily lead to a feeling of being undeserving of anything good, because he had enough of a conscience to realize it was wrong, even though he felt compelled to continue to attempt to please his father. But far worse was the sense that, no matter how well he did, he never would succeed because he had never been a success in his father's eyes. And besides, Jack didn't deserve any of his success anyway. Not just because of his adolescent thuggish behavior, but mostly because his father had drilled into his head that he was a first-class screwup.

When Jack married, he went straight. Although a high school dropout, he and his ambitious wife started an honest business that was worth $3 million and growing. Still Jack felt like an undeserving and worthless failure. Despite their obvious success, he regularly sabotaged himself by not going in to work if he didn't feel like it. Instead, he would sleep away the day or smoke marijuana to dull the pain. But there was always a part of him that wanted to do good and do well. He routinely donated his time and his company's resources to people in need. It was not until we began to work with the father's own unworthiness, which he had passed along by projection and drummed into Jack's head, that Jack finally could claim his success. And finally, when he was able to stop needing it so desperately, Jack got his father's acknowledgment that he had done some things right.

Feeling Abandoned by the Higher Power

The spiritual issue generated for people who experience father loss typically is some version of the question "If my earthly father abandoned me, how can I believe that a higher power—or anyone else—will stay?" This theme is a companion theme to the one of being undeserving. As if it is not bad enough to be abandoned by an earthly parent, to feel what is interpreted as the higher power's abandonment by silence is deafening. It also can be terrorizing and disillusioning.

It takes wisdom and courage to believe, as Nobel laureate Elie Wiesel did, even after his harrowing experiences in four different concentration camps during World War II. In addition to his own internment in the Nazi death camps, Wiesel had to endure never again seeing his mother and sister, who were snatched from him and sent to another camp, and his father nearly dying at Buchenwald before the liberation. All of this as an adolescent! Rather than trying to control God or becoming cynical because of the events he witnessed daily as a young boy in the camps, he chose to believe, as I now do, that God suffers when people suffer. In that sense, people do not need to wait for their "final reward" to experience the presence of God. In his autobiographical account of life and death in the prisons, Wiesel wrote of his conclusion, eloquently voicing the anguish of millions who grieve over or rail about the seeming absence of God in the Holocaust.

> One day when we came back from work, we saw three gallows rearing up in the assembly place. Three victims in chains—and one of them the little servant, the sad-eyed angel. Three victims were mounted together onto chairs. The three necks were placed at the same moment within nooses. At a sign, the three chairs tipped over. Total silence throughout the camp. Then the march past began. The two adults were no longer alive. But the third rope was still moving; being so light, the child was still alive. For more than half an hour he stayed there, struggling between life and death, dying in slow

agony under our eyes. And we had to look him full in the face. Behind me I heard a man asking: "Where is God now?" and I heard a voice within me answer him: "Where is God? Here — God is hanging here on this gallows."[6]

God's promise, and the only real consolation to be hoped for, is the sense of with-ness that Wiesel describes and that I finally came to know. The belief that one's higher power is present even in the most horrific experiences—and especially then—can itself be consoling and healing. Thus, the belief in God's presence can spawn a ripple effect. Not having to grieve alone may help people believe that they have not been abandoned again, as well as have faith that if they must endure another loss, they can survive it because they do not have to cope alone. What can people rely on? A God who is a fellow sufferer, who understands and comforts those who feel hurt or alone. And when people can rely on a higher power to be there, it is much more possible to believe that a mere mortal will also be.

Difficulty Trusting

The most common damage I see as a result of being unable to answer the spiritual questions involved in a loss occurs in the area of trust. It is very difficult to trust an earthly companion or parent if one's heavenly companion seems like the enemy! Conversely, if people can come to believe that God can be trusted to be with them in their struggle to cope with loss, then it is much more likely that they can see people as benign companions. Most people would acknowledge having difficulty asking for help from someone they do not trust. However, trusting again after a loss is extremely difficult for anyone. Many, rather than making a leap of faith to trust in both a higher power and a partner, continue to test their mate's trustworthiness long after it is warranted or appropriate. This may be based on the unconscious belief that if God is untrustworthy, how can people be trusted?

The spouse or child of someone who has not adequately resolved the question of trusting has the flip side of the dilemma from their partner or parent, even if that person has experienced no particular trauma. Since trust is both courageous and contagious, the mate's problem is how to trust someone who is so untrusting. Thus, a disease of mistrust and suspicion pervades and eventually compromises the relationship.

Scott was in his early forties when he sustained an injury on the job in an accident caused by someone else's negligence. Although the accident caused a 27 percent permanent physical disability for Scott, that was not the worst part. What hurt the most was that his highly authoritarian boss, whom Scott came to think of as a father figure, blamed Scott for the accident and for his injuries. Scott was devastated. Then he unknowingly compounded his own agony by how he handled the accident, his injuries and the spiritual and then relationship crises that followed.

Previously a pious, strong, fundamentalist believer, now Scott railed at the God that his religious tradition and his beliefs had constructed. How could he have allowed these events to happen? Further, he kept demanding that God prove himself trustworthy. Then and only then would Scott take the risk to believe again. And because he had decided that God had betrayed him by allowing the accident, it followed that his wife also inevitably would betray him. Although she had done nothing to warrant it, he came to treat her as if she were the devil personified. His entire self-protective armor, of course, only intensified his problems. But he couldn't see that, and it was my job to help him do so. Only then could he become an instrument of his own healing instead of continuing the swath of destruction.

In an ill-fated effort to try to resolve his dilemma, Scott kept setting up challenges for God to meet in order to be worthy of Scott's renewed faith and love. Apparently, his fantasy was that if he could control God and get him to pass Scott's tests and jump through Scott's hoops, then it would be safe to trust. Until then, he would trust no one and nothing. Then, he thought, he could ensure that he would not be abandoned again. You can imagine what a therapeutic task it was for me to eventually gain Scott's trust!

What are the elements of father loss that made Scott a candidate for such extremes of suspicion and mistrust? Although Scott's father was a physician whose life's work was healing, he was savage when it came to Scott. He frequently and sadistically beat Scott for real or imagined imperfections. The times he "only" berated and verbally abused Scott seemed like welcome relief to the boy because there were no bruises to hide, and because at least he had some shards of the man's attention. The oldest of six children, Scott learned from an early age that he could not trust his father and that the only way he could avoid abuse was to be perfect. As that was not possible for any human to do, Scott's accident had rendered him permanently flawed. In Scott's mind, he was unworthy, unlovable and permanently unable to attain perfection because he was permanently disabled. His only recourse was to hide his flaws, which he did by extremely rigid defenses.

Of course, then he was hiding from everyone including himself. Moreover, all of these experiences made it impossible for his to see his heavenly father as trustworthy as well.

Forgiving God for Lacking Omnipotence in the Crisis

In addition to admitting anger at God for the losses people have sustained, perhaps the other most frightening spiritual issue that must be resolved is forgiving God for not being omnipotent. If people are not already angry with God for a loss, many become angry because they expected his omnipotence to prevent it, just as they unconsciously expect their earthly father to protect them. It is natural to wish and to hope that God will take care of us and shield us from bad things happening to good people, and that we will live in a Promised Land where no change will happen without our permission.[7] But I see this belief as an earmark of immature faith. God's apparent silence in the face of human tragedy seems unnecessary and inexcusable if God is viewed as omnipotent.

My own construct of God now is that he is not omnipotent. Otherwise, there simply would not be horrible events such as those that took place in the Holocaust of World War II, famine and pediatric cancer. God would prevent them. Perhaps the most difficult spiritual issue to discern the answer to is why tragedies happen and what people are to learn from them.

If we cannot forgive God, it is difficult to see how there can be the requisite forgiveness of self or others, particularly our own father. Moreover, this unwillingness to forgive not only stymies our own growth, but it also makes healing the wounds we inevitably inflict on others out of our imperfect humanness difficult at best, impossible at worst. The Reverend Carla Bailey addressed this need in a sermon entitled "RADS in

Our Milk and Honey," shortly after the Chernobyl nuclear accident in Russia. The following is an excerpt.

> Forgiving God is an issue we must tiptoe around so often. It's just not right somehow, thinking of forgiving God—as if we had the right to do it. But I will tell you something—the deafening silence of God in human tragedy is a transgression for which, though I may not have the right to forgive, I have to come to a willingness to forgive or my faith stops cold and leaves me empty. If I could choose to feel differently about God at those times, I would, but for whatever reason, the deepest challenge to my believing is forgiving God for silence as freely as I praise God for music.[8]

It is presumptuous to think that we mortals know better than God. There is also arrogance in seeing forgiveness as something we must do. If we can start seeing it as something we must be, then we will benefit ourselves as well as those who need and deserve our forgiveness.

Conclusion

The central task that comes with resolving each of these spiritual issues is learning to trust, even in the face of subsequent losses that are inevitable elements of the human condition. Fathers have a unique role with respect to trust issues, as we have seen. For some, that means recovering the willingness to trust. For others, this means learning to trust at all. Whatever the case, this is an essential part of healing and of allowing ourselves to be transformed.

The subject of spirituality is gaining greater and greater acceptance. This is apparent in the immense popularity of books like *The Celestine Prophecy* and *Conversations with God,* and authors like Deepak Chopra, Caroline Myss and Joan Borysenko. Still, it is a topic that can be fraught with risk. Those whose spiritual struggle is just outside their awareness are particularly in jeopardy. If they cannot surface and resolve the spiritual issues inherent in any trauma, they likely are doomed to remain stuck by and in it. Thus, spiritual issues are often at the heart of why acute father loss becomes chronic and unresolved. When people cannot make a meaningful spiritual connection of some sort with their higher power, they do not have this powerful resource to help them heal. When they can, they have help to endure the seemingly unendurable.

References

1. Caroline Myss. *Anatomy of the Spirit: The Seven Stages of Power and Healing* (Boulder, Colorado: Sounds True Audio, 1996).

2. Ira Progoff, *At a Journal Workshop: The Basic Text and Guide for Using the Intensive Journal* (New York: Dialogue House Library, 1975).

3. Charme Davidson, "Blocks to Intimacy: The Synergy of Unresolved Loss" (unpublished manuscript, 1989).

4. Viktor Frankl, *Man's Search for Meaning: An Introduction to Logotherapy* (New York: Washington Square Press, 1959).

5. C. S. Lewis, *A Grief Observed* (New York: Bantam Books, 1961), 15.

6. Elie Wiesel, *Night* (New York: Bantam Books, 1960), 61-62.

7. Myss, *Anatomy of the Spirit.*

8. Carla Bailey, "RADs in Our Milk and Honey" (Plymouth Congregational Church, Minneapolis, Minn., 29 June 1986).

PART THREE

Remedies and Recovery

8 Taking the Bite Out of Father Hunger

*Bless this pain for it will bear its perfect
gift to you in its perfect time.*

—Rusty Berkus
*To Heal Again: Towards Serenity
and the Resolution of Grief*

If you have read this far, you are probably prepared to acknowledge that unresolved father
loss is a factor in your life, either for you or a
loved one. For some, the pain has been a dull ache
that most of the time they manage to tune out, as one
does Muzak in an elevator. But this chapter is for
you who want to resolve your pain and be free of it.

What I Am Not Saying

Simply because I offer suggestions for the
management and resolution of father loss does *not*

mean that I believe its resolution is a one-size-fits-all proposition. Nor do I believe that this book is a cookbook containing the recipe for ending misery—or that such a formula even exists. Rather, it is important for people to discover what works for them. As Rusty Berkus wrote in her beautifully illustrated book, "There is no right way to grieve—there is just Your way. It will take as long as it takes."[1] I sincerely hope to help you generate options for shucking the relics of your past that haunt you, so that you can move on instead of merely continuing to step over these compelling, antiquated experiences.

Veronica: "Please Help Me Understand What Happened"

Forty-four-year-old Veronica began therapy to recover from an acrimonious marriage and a stormy divorce. She wanted to ensure that she did not repeat her disastrous mistakes or inflict them on her children. As the crisis of her divorce began to subside and we were able to search for the factors that drew her into such an abusive marriage, we did not have to look far. Veronica was the oldest of five children who grew up in a lower-middle-class household. Her father was a college graduate who earned a modest living, and her mother was a homemaker. Veronica's father was the oldest of eleven children whose own father, according to her, became a "wicked, bad alcoholic" who would go on three-day drunks and steal the family's money meant for medicine to buy liquor. So Veronica's father became the family's "little man," soon taking the responsibility of supporting the family. Clearly, Veronica's father had no childhood himself, so he was at a loss regarding how to protect his children's childhoods.

Because of their family's modest financial means, Veronica and her siblings were deprived of opportunities that Veronica's own children now take for granted. But being deprived of protection and security were far worse for her. That, and the amorphous feeling that somehow she was both evil and, worse yet, invisible, became unbearable for her. And it took us a long time to identify the factors that made her feel that way.

Gradually, unbidden and disturbing memories began to float to the surface. First, Veronica remembered that she had been raped in her early twenties. Then she realized that as a preschooler, three older neighborhood boys had molested her. Remembering, in turn, set in motion a trickle of even more disturbing memories. At first, those recollections were neither pictures nor stories. They came first in the form of strange physiological sensations, particularly when she was lying in bed. It took her a while to identify the sensation. It was a man's erect penis pressing against her from behind. This in turn spawned a cascade of memories. Of the times her father would stumble drunk into her bed because her mother had locked their bedroom door. Of his standing outside his own locked bedroom door at night, drunk and pitifully begging his wife to open it. Of the times he stumbled to the doorway of Veronica's room at night and leered at her until she awoke. Of the times he called her by her mother's name and heaved his heavy arm across her in bed in his drunken stupor. Of his sometimes passing out on the couch and her feeling guilty for having escaped, at least for that night. Of her siblings' puzzlement about and resentment of the special attention she got from their father.

Fear frequently goes hand in hand with the retrieval of such disturbing memories. It is natural for people to worry that such discoveries will have catastrophic implications for them and for their families. So this phase of Veronica's treatment was painstakingly slow. Veronica's biggest challenge was to continue to allow her denial to thaw so she could know and face the stark truth of her childhood. And mine was managing not to become impatient while she appropriately kept her foot on both the accelerator and the brake of treatment. Clearly, she was moving at the pace that she was able to go and still be assured that she could keep life together for herself and her four children in elementary school.

Finally, after probing, planning and procrastinating for months, she came into a session with a draft of the letter to her parents she had promised both of us she would write. Because her father was a practicing alcoholic, we agreed that communicating in writing, at least to broach the subject, was the most promising. This way, he could read the letter when the mail came early in the day, when he still likely would be sober. And the parents both could reread the letter as they wished and needed, giving them an opportunity to give her a more deliberate, less reactive response. It also allowed her to be clear about her newly acquired understandings of how these unfortunate situations happened, rather than to accuse or blame either parent. Her letter follows.

Dear Mom and Dad,

I have wanted to take the opportunity to air some of my feelings with you both, as I think it may help us to all come to a better understanding of one another. I have been angry for a long time about some things that happened a long time ago. It would be wonderful for me to be able to put these issues to rest. When we visit one another, I invariably end up angry about things that usually don't matter that much to me—I believe these other issues are at the root of my anger. I would love [us] to be able to visit each other and to simply have a nice time. These issues won't be news to either of you as you both were there, but perhaps you have forgotten, as a long time has passed and it may not have impacted your life as much as it has mine.

When I was a teenager, sometimes Dad would come into my bedroom to sleep at night. I'm not sure what all of the dynamics were—issues between the two of you, alcohol—I don't know. Those issues are not what this letter is about. It was very confusing for me to have Dad sleeping in my room with me. I do not remember that anything much happened. I do remember that Dad called me [Mom's name] a few times, that he needed comforting for some reason that really is not mine to figure out, either.

This was a very inappropriate situation. I feel that not only were sexual issues clouded for me, but that I wasn't well taken care of in this regard. I should have been able to feel that I had privacy that was respected and that I was safe and protected. Dad, you should have not been sleeping in my room, and Mom, you should have gotten me out of that situation. I don't know what was going on in our home or between the two of you that this circumstance was allowed, ignored or tolerated. Again, those issues seem to belong to the two of you. Perhaps I'm wrong. I don't know.

I do know that I feel a fundamental disrespect from you both and I believe that this issue is among the issues at the core of this disrespect. I was a child, truly. A teenager, but still a child. I feel that I was treated as though I had done something wrong, had been sexually promiscuous, inappropriately alluring.

I have never been sexually promiscuous. If I behaved in an alluring manner, it was because I seemed to learn that that was how I could gain [the] attention that I felt I needed. I am no longer concerned about those implications. I am concerned about the basic events that occurred, and I would appreciate it if you could share anything you could about your memories of these events. I particularly would like to know that you are sorry that this happened, and for the confusion it caused within me.

I know that you are both very proud of me and love me very much. I love you both, too. I would really like to be able to move past [the] feelings of anger, disrespect, sadness and separation I feel surrounding these issues. I believe that I have to air this issue to move past those feelings.

It is not my intention to hurt either of you, to stir up old problems or to create more distance between us or between you. I truly want to have a closer, more adult relationship with you. I love you both, and I'm so proud of you as my parents and for all of the wonderful things you have taught me about life, about important values and about people. I would really like to get past this.

I love you both,

—Veronica

There are at least a dozen factors that make Veronica's letter constructive.

1. She did not blame, accuse or sound defensive.
2. She installed a boundary between herself, her parents and their marriage.
3. She affirmed her own reality, not giving it away while she asked her parents to be clear about theirs.
4. She took responsibility for her own feelings.

5. She asked her parents to take responsibility for both their actions and for failing to act.

6. She took responsibility to articulate what she wanted and needed from her parents now.

7. She made concrete suggestions about what they could do to make restitution.

8. She told both parents that her reason for writing was to ask for help.

9. She affirmed her love for and gratitude toward both parents.

10. She clarified that her intention and desired outcome in bringing up this difficult topic were to put it behind them and to improve their relationship, not to hurt her parents.

11. Although she did not specifically refer to events in the past of either parent that might account for this family's sad state of affairs, the tone of the letter was one of empathy for them, rather than condemnation.

12. Her request gave them an opportunity to parent her now, and to attempt to make up for their mutual and multiple shortcomings when she was a child.

Of course, there is no formula that everyone must follow in composing such a letter. Those contemplating the use of this strategy will need to factor in their knowledge of the cast of characters in their own situation. When adult children honestly and genuinely can state their reality, feelings and needs *as well as acknowledge the parent's perspective,* they can initiate a process that greatly enhances the chances of healing for all. Truly, this stance has the best chance of opening a dialogue with parents, if anything will. Said David Viscott, "Taking responsibility for everything in your life gives you the power to change it. Taking responsibility for nothing ensures that you'll stay a victim."[2] I could not agree more.

Some Words of Caution

There are several special considerations that readers who believe they are ready to resolve their father loss must keep in mind. Being aware of these caveats gives them the best possible chance to accomplish this laudable goal.

Companions for the Journey

There are many sorts of companions who can be helpful. Some of you will seek the training and experience of a competent therapist. Others will meet periodically with a member of the clergy or a spiritual director. Still others will link in with a best friend or spouse for periodic check-ins and support. And others will go it alone, with just a journal as a companion. Make your decision based on what works best for you. Regardless of the route you choose, it is essential to make this odyssey to become whole. Any one of these options can provide bread for the journey.

When Adult Children's Issues
Collide with Their Father's

There is a good chance that, if you experience father loss, unless it is due to his death, your father suffers from it as well. Otherwise, he likely would have had the tools to be a different parent. Therefore, it would be reasonable to expect some resistance on his part to discussing the sensitive topic of his unavailability. Just as a spouse's emotions often trigger unwanted and unwelcome feelings, your sharing likely will stir your father's dormant feelings as well. And equally likely, he may not understand or know what to do with them or you. So it would be wise, at least initially, to expect defensiveness on his part and yours, and to plan a strategy for how to deal with it.

If your family history suggests that your father suffered his own father loss from one of the seven sources discussed in chapter 4, you would be wise not to be surprised if your father's initial response to your probes falls at one extreme or the other. He either may put up his own wall and have a reserved and even stony reaction. Or he may be testy or even explosive. In most instances, this will not be because he does not care; rather, it will be because his child's issues have slammed into his own. At least initially, he may respond defensively to hide feelings of inadequacy as his shortcomings as a parent are pointed out. To ensure that the attempt to open communication does not run amok, it may be safest to meet with your father in the presence of a therapist. That way, both father and child have an interpreter to help minimize the potential for misunderstandings that could damage instead of strengthen your already tenuous relationship. I will offer a detailed discussion of the logistics of such a meeting in appendix B.

Choosing the Right Therapist

The findings of a classic piece of research on the major ingredients of effective counseling regardless of a therapist's particular theoretical orientation are relevant here.[3] The researchers' conclusion was that warmth, genuineness, and empathy are essential attributes of a successful and effective

therapist. Obviously, it is possible and desirable that all therapists possess these attributes, regardless of their theoretical
orientation. If you are not currently in therapy, I urge you to
select a therapist who would work in the ways listed below.
Regardless of their theoretical orientation, therapists who are
likely to be helpful on this issue would:

1. Work collaboratively, preferring to do therapy *with* you
   rather than *on* you;
2. Be comfortable with the expression of strong feelings;
3. See the process as a journey to embark on, rather than
   as a solution to focus on;
4. Help you creatively evolve what needs to be done,
   rather than operating out of a formula they superimpose
   or a preconceived notion of what you should do;
5. Not assume that your father loss is something you just
   should put behind you, but rather see it as a process to
   work through;
6. Preferably have dealt with their own losses;
7. Understand at least the basics of family dynamics;
8. Not seek to blame or to find a "bad guy," because
   fathers in this situation are easy targets;
9. Be able to see the parents' perspective despite and while
   maintaining their alliance with you;
10. Have no ax to grind with his or her own parents that will
    spill over onto you or your parents.

It is important to choose a therapist who is sensitive to
deeper issues and has a willingness to wade into emotions with
you. Otherwise, merely treating people's infidelity, obesity,

backaches or headaches will not solve the problem in the long run. Perhaps missing the mark on these deeper issues accounts in part for the revolving door of mental health services that so many decry. Be an informed consumer and ask questions of potential therapists that would help determine whether they are willing to work in the ways outlined.

The biggest danger of choosing a therapist who turns out to be ineffective, at least on this issue, is that you might then legitimately expect that you have done what you need to do. Countless times, I have heard people who obviously still have broken hearts say that they have been in therapy and that therapy does no good. Worse yet is the situation where clients, in the beginning of treatment, say that they have talked *about* their issues many times in previous therapies. Yet, it is obvious to both of us that they are still stuck. This problem develops when both therapist and client believe that talking *about* an issue amounts to dealing with it. It does not. Intellectualization is a powerful defense, and men, because of their socialization, particularly can fall prey to it. Empty insights without putting feelings with them freeze people into "analysis paralysis," where all the understandings in the world have done nothing to dislodge the boulders of their defenses. *Although certainly new insights and understandings are important, only putting them with the feelings that accompany them will resolve the issue.*

Your Mother, or Father's New Wife, as Guardian of the Status Quo

As I discussed in chapter 6, all families are a system. Each develops its own synergy that governs everyone's ways of relating with each other and with the outside world. The equilibrium that some families develop can make them impenetrable by outsiders and impervious to change. For others, change is a welcome and accepted reality, the yeast in the bread of life. The more rigid and dysfunctional the family, the greater stake its members will have in keeping it the same and in keeping out those whose presence represents change.

Any family member can serve as a system regulator, or homeostat. However, readers who attempt to change their relationship with their father may run into a brick wall in the form of their own mother or their father's present wife. Although theoretically it is possible that this woman assumes the role of homeostat out of malicious intent, more likely it is because she feels protective of her husband and of their present environment. This is particularly a risk if the father and mother of the adult child are no longer together. His new wife likely will have little or no loyalty or even attachment to his children from his former life. Instead, she can be expected to have (and should have) a much greater commitment to her husband. She may feel compelled to intervene for him and in the service of the balance in the new family. So she likely will align with her husband and try to protect him if she thinks his child is ready to attack. Particularly mothers of dysfunctional families can act like the mythical Cerberus at the gates of hell, allowing only certain people in. In these instances, for you to approach your father without a therapist as an ally would be like Daniel in the lion's den. Rather than for you to give up on building a different and better relationship with your father, it would be essential for you to seek the input and support of a professional in planning and even executing such a meeting. The therapist can help you make sure that you don't get ground up in your family's unconscious and automatic wish to protect the status quo and to elect those who threaten it.

Conversation, Not Confrontation

The mind-set with which you approach opening a dialogue with your father, regardless of whether you do so on paper, alone and in person, on the phone or in a therapist's office is essential to your success. *If you envision yourself confronting your father, you are not yet ready to take on this task.*

You are probably still too angry or defensive to dialogue constructively. By contrast, *having the mental set of initiating a conversation with him has the greatest potential to yield a better, more honest relationship.* When you are ready to share the range of your feelings with your father and to invite him to do the same, then you are properly prepared—*and not until then.*

Does this mean that you should not confess your anger to your father? Absolutely not! The key is *how it is expressed and with what intent.* If feeling angry and being unable to express it contribute to your internal logjam and the distance between your father and you, disclosing anger not only is acceptable, but also is essential. If revealing feelings is done to improve the relationship by being honest and by putting festering feelings to rest, it likely will be constructive. If, however, the intent is to blast him or to seek revenge, it is highly unlikely that this will get you the fathering you want, need and deserve. If you feel vindictive, you are not ready to have this conversation. You will not be ready to deal with your father until you have dealt with yourself. Although vengeful feelings are perfectly normal when you have been wronged, if you wish to preserve a relationship rather than to kill it, you must work through these feelings and set them aside. Part of the purpose of this honest conversation is to ask for your father's help in getting through the hurt. Otherwise, forgiveness is impossible.

How to Tell When a Loss Is Resolved

Workshop participants and my own clients consistently ask me how we will know when a loss is resolved. For years, my cryptic answer was, "We'll know." That answer seems to satisfy some people. But others need a more specific answer. Here are a baker's dozen signs that tell me that father loss is resolved:

1. The symptoms that are evidence of this festering problem have subsided or disappeared.
2. The emotional charge that so often accompanies a discussion of this issue is gone.
3. You feel unburdened and others notice that you are.
4. Your emotional roller-coaster stops, and your overall feeling state becomes more moderated and modulated.
5. You either have overhauled your relationship with your father or have come genuinely (not just intellectually) to accept that it will not be different.
6. You have learned a genuine acceptance of what happened—or didn't.
7. You can discuss what happened without finding fault or blaming.
8. You have incorporated the meaning of the loss into your life and are truly ready to move beyond it.
9. You feel changed as a result of your journey.
10. You no longer are preoccupied with past events.
11. You no longer feel like a victim.
12. You feel, and are, in control of your life without being controlling.

13. You have more energy for living because of the release of all the effort it took to keep your powerful feelings repressed and unresolved.

This list is not intended to be all-inclusive, and readers are encouraged to add their own ideas.

How Approachable Are Fathers?

I have observed five categories of responses that fathers typically make.

Fathers who are receptive but relationally inept: These fathers are the easiest to work with because they generally can respond in a relatively nondefensive way. They are likely to grasp the meaning of their child's request and the depth of the hurt, even if they do not immediately know what to do. These fathers can be taught relatively easily to respond appropriately either by the adult child or a therapist. Examples of such simple statements are "Dad, it would really help if you would say X" or "I need you to do Y." Because these fathers are the most open despite their awkwardness, it probably would not be precarious for adult children to approach them in an informal one-on-one meeting. Still, however, I would urge those who expect their fathers to fall into this category to be deliberate, rather than impulsive, in meeting with him. Even with this kind of father, having a plan will maximize the chances of achieving the optimal outcome.

Fathers who are resistant to relationships because of their own unresolved losses and intimacy fears: The first response of these fathers will likely be defensiveness. This is because any discussion of the losses their parenting created has the risk of taking them back to their own unresolved father loss. So it can be more difficult to get a helpful and healing response from them. There are multiple ways their defensiveness could manifest.

A common defense is anger. Fathers who immediately fly off the handle and cannot or will not calm down are stuck in their own agenda to protect themselves, rather than to respond. They wish, however unconsciously, to keep their own loss where it has always been: out of sight and out of mind. They have great difficulty seeing past their own needs and defenses to grasp what their child needs. And they always have.

Another common defense is apparent disinterest. These fathers have withdrawn from their children so far that nothing short of their suicide will get his attention. Still another defense is to shift the responsibility to the child. This comes in many forms, not the least of which is blaming the children for being ungrateful for what he did do. Approaching these fathers is risky. So readers are urged not to do so without the help, preferably of a therapist, but at least that of a spouse or close friend. They need to be certain that they are clear on what they need to say and be willing to stand their ground calmly but firmly. Otherwise, they may be bullied or ignored into stuffing their concerns once again.

Narcissistically self-absorbed fathers: These fathers are dangerous because they are involved with no one but themselves. They will hold court only with those who will adore them. These fathers must come across as perfect at all costs, even and especially when they are not. So a discussion of mistakes they made or of what was missing is extremely precarious because of the threat that they might have to see their own imperfections. These fathers deftly dodge taking responsibility for their actions or inaction unless a therapist helps hold their feet to the fire. Otherwise, blame for their children's pain will probably get shifted back to the child. Blaming and faultfinding characterize many interactions because such fathers are unable to take what they perceive as criticism. Dumping on others allows them to continue their delusions of adequacy. These parents have the narcissistic tendency to see their children as objects who are reflections of themselves. If parents are not too rigidly defended by their self-absorption, they can be helped to respond to what their children need with coaching, usually from a therapist. But other parents, true narcissists according to psychologist Elana Golomb, are more impervious to their children's needs—or anyone else's, for that matter. In her powerful book *Trapped in the Mirror: Adult Children of Narcissists in Their Struggle for Self*, she wrote, "The child of a [true] narcissist is not supposed to see her own power. . . . Credit to the self interferes with obedience to the law: Be nothing."[4]

Children of narcissistic parents must develop numerous defenses in an effort to survive psychologically. You must become "psychologically hard of hearing," deafening yourself as a defense against your parent's attributing to you what is unacceptable in the parent.[5] Narcissists must always be right. If you grew up with a steady diet of being wrong and bad, before long, you began to believe this very powerful person's messages. Despite attempts to deflect your parent's annihilating messages, some still penetrated, and you ended up internalizing some of these crushing, denigrating statements. These zingers then became part of your own inner dialogue. It is easy to see the extreme delicacy of approaching these types of fathers with the wish for greater honesty and emotional connection in the relationship. This does not mean, however, that facing him is not a good idea. It is. At the very least, when you finally speak your truth, you can begin to extricate yourself from your narcissistic father's clutches. If you believe your father falls into this category, I urge you to seek therapeutic help both to determine whether or not this is the case, and to craft a plan for how to proceed. Even if a conversation is only another reiteration of your father's rationalized self-interest, at least you will have tried everything. There is no more to do but to disconnect and grieve the fathering you never had and never will have.

Fathers impaired by addictions: They are often close but so far away. Particularly if their condition is not being addressed somehow, relating to these fathers can be precarious indeed. If they are not in treatment, consider doing a family intervention so that they have no choice but to at least hear that they have a problem. It is important to note, however, that unless that father is a danger to himself or others, treatment cannot be compelled. In these instances, the comments in the final paragraph of this section apply. If your father is a practicing addict, it would be wise to plan contact with him at times when he is most likely to be sober. But you probably have known that for years!

Fathers who are mentally ill: It is virtually impossible to get a clear picture of reality from them and with them because they see everything egocentrically and idiosyncratically and without regard to objective reality. This is problematic enough because their skewed or twisted views generally render them emotionally unavailable. But worse yet, most insist that others who want to relate to them adopt their distorted views as well. Any divergent view is experienced as an attack. But probably the most damaging aspect of their parenting is their attempt, however unconsciously, to wipe out both your perceptions and your attempts to develop an independent self. Suggestions for how to approach these sorts of fathers are the same as those I made for true narcissists. But because it's unlikely to achieve a quality relationship with someone who lives in his own world—especially if he is not being treated or has taken himself off his medication—perhaps the only recourse is to attempt to treat the condition. The only other option is to grieve. In these unfortunate situations, there are three losses that must be worked with: the losses that resulted from the fathering you had; the losses that occurred from the fathering you did not have; and the losses from the fathering you never will have.

Some Final Thoughts on Fathers' Availability

Gauging a father's emotional availability is one of the most important aspects of preparation to approach him with the request for a new kind of relationship. Because this can be a rather subtle process of discernment, if you feel your father cannot be helped to become emotionally available, it would be wise to consult with a family therapist in order to make certain that this conclusion does not arise out of sheer defensiveness on either of your parts. Even if you decide to have the conversation with your father by yourself, the coaching of a professional can be invaluable preparation. Their job then becomes helping you assess the realities of your situation, develop a strategy and prepare for potential pitfalls. I will elaborate more on this at the end of the book.

Most fathers know that something is missing in their relationship with their children; it is likely that they have missed the relationship, too. This can be particularly poignant as parents age and move into the developmental stage that involves a life review. So unless fathers are highly narcissistic or otherwise mentally ill, they likely would welcome the chance for a better relationship, but they just don't know how to achieve one. Those fathers simply will need help figuring out what needs to be done.

Do Not Bury a Living Father

Finally, although it may be tempting to do, it is not advisable to grieve a father who is living as though he were dead. Yet, for too many, having a totally unavailable father is tantamount to his being dead. And though it seems easier to carry on as if he were dead, in the long run, it is not. Instead, you need to acknowledge that your father's unavailability, whatever the cause, is a significant and painful loss, and attention must be paid. To resolve this loss and to prepare for his eventual dying, grieve the father you needed but will never have. Then, when your father dies, you can stand at his coffin free of regrets. Finishing what you can before your father dies by accepting his limitations enables you not to languish hoping for more, when what you need is not and never will be forthcoming. But it also allows you to acknowledge any tidbits of fathering you did get.

Suggestions for Resolving the Loss

The following is a list of some tried-and-true strategies for resolving father loss. Some of them have been referred to in case studies sprinkled throughout the book. The less complicated tactics for resolving loss will be described briefly in this chapter. The most involved and technical ones will be reserved for the appendix for therapists. None of these suggestions is likely to be potent enough to totally resolve a loss. Would that it could! Therefore, readers need to expect to use several of these in combination.

Journaling: Writing in a journal is talking to yourself on paper. In this way, you can become your own therapist. I routinely recommend this strategy to clients whatever their issue. Purchase a blank book with an inviting cover and a comfortable format to record your passage on this arduous and exciting journey. Its being appealing will serve as an incentive to sit down daily—or several times a day—to check in with yourself via the journal. Doing so gives you an opportunity to get thoughts and feelings out of the closed feedback loop in your head and onto paper, where you can objectively evaluate them. It also serves as a container for strong feelings that surface. When the journal's cover is closed, the roller-coaster of feelings that are an inevitable part of this process can be held in a safe place. Then you won't be so afraid of being overwhelmed and overpowered by emotions, and you won't have the temptation to rationalize and keep your defenses intact. Seeing your reflections on paper also gives greater objectivity and the opportunity to find out what you really think and feel instead of how you think you are supposed to respond.

Occasionally rereading entries will allow you to chart your progress on the journey as well as to identify persistent themes and patterns that are reflected back in your musings. Journaling is second only to the therapy hour in potency and potential for change, so I highly recommend both tools.

Paint, sculpt or write poetry: Having a creative outlet for emotions can help you stop intellectualizing and get out of your head. Each of these tools can be used as a kind of tribute to your father or an expression of the father you lost or never had. Like journaling, these methods can be used as a channel for strong emotions so that there is a safe place to put them. It also helps in giving amorphous feelings some shape and form, thereby bringing order out of internal chaos.

Make a collage: Like the three suggestions just listed, preparing a collage offers a creative outlet for strong emotions. But it has the additional benefit of helping those people who feel fragmented or have significant pieces missing to put scattered parts of themselves in place. This literally helps bring order out of internal chaos. It also offers an easy way to get out of your conscious mind and tune in to messages from the unconscious. To do a collage, simply thumb through magazines, looking for pictures, words and phrases that speak to you from the pages. Don't think too much, just *do*. Don't try to give it form or to find a way to organize it until doing so feels right. Then, mount your clippings and do "show-and-tell" with a concerned other.

Write letters that are never sent: Sometimes acting "as if" is enough. The mere process of writing a letter, if doing so is accompanied by the expression of emotions, can be cathartic. Writing letters never sent allows people to get everything off their chest without worrying about how it is going to be received—because it never will be. Simply finding the words to articulate long dormant thoughts and feelings is itself an important step in getting closure and healing.

Send letters and follow up: If your father is available to talk, write a letter as a door opener, stating that you will follow up with a telephone call. Usually, the purpose of such a phone call is to arrange an in-person discussion. But if distance or other circumstances make meeting impossible, an extended telephone call will have to suffice. Since it is better that both of you be prepared and have set aside ample time, the first phone call is merely to make arrangements for the longer meeting, whether it is to be on the phone or in person.

Photo therapy: A picture is worth a thousand words for learning about what shaped a father's reactions to you. Whether working with a therapist or flying solo, studying old family photographs can be very enlightening and cathartic. Doing so can prompt hypotheses about how your father was fathered, so you appropriately can depersonalize his lack of attention to you. Also, you can begin to draw inferences from photos about family patterns that would be a factor in molding your and your father's lives. Another advantage—if fragmentary experiences with your father left you with major and many holes in your identity—is that reconnecting with extended family by photo or in person can help you knit yourself together. Study any old family photos you can access, not limiting yourself to pictures of your father. The idea is to clarify new understandings cognitively and to reach for feelings that accompany them.

Collect information from other family members: This strategy is closely related to the one just listed. Often, particularly if your father has vanished, you have great knowledge gaps about him that only information will fill. Missing data about someone as significant as a father causes gaps in children's psyches. So acquiring information, no matter how trivial it seems, will help them fill in the cracks. This is why family reunions are important, even if meeting Great Aunt Selma and Great Uncle Henry seems boring.

Revisit your childhood home, neighborhood or family burial plot: The usefulness of this is obvious if your father is dead. If he is unknown but his family or their cemetery can be found, making a pilgrimage there can still provide vital pieces of your internal puzzle. Just seeing the tombstones and noting the information found on them can seem like a mainline to the self. Being able to say, "These are my people" helps develop or bolster a sense of belonging. Likewise, you may want to revisit your childhood home, even if strangers now occupy it. And walking through old neighborhoods is also a way to connect with a larger sense of family and with your past. Doing so also helps shake emotions loose. Take pictures of these sojourns. Photos will serve as a silent witness, will help you not forget and will be a valuable ingredient of your legacy for any children you have or might have.

I intuited that reenacting a burial ceremony for my Dad twenty-four years after he died would be life changing, and truly it was. Daddy was hospitalized in mid-September and died in early November, and since then, I had been moderately depressed as every fall approached. Of course, I had no conscious knowledge of the genesis of this malaise until I began working to resolve his death, because I long ago had repressed awareness of the significance of these events. I had even "forgotten" the dates! As fall again approached the year Dorothy died, I sensed that I could give myself the gift of freedom. I also knew that, once I recognized the unresolved grief I had for my father, I was not going to be able to get the genie back in the bottle. Finally having an explanation for the melancholy that plagued me every fall since I could remember, I resolved to get closure. I also was determined not to slide into that old, familiar groove of denial with either his or my sister's death.

On the anniversary of Dad's actual funeral, a trusted friend and I carried out a ritual that I now think of as his funeral. Since I had stumbled numbly through his funeral the first time and because a child's mind simply cannot comprehend death, now I finally could "bury" him. I culminated this commemoration with a trip to Minnesota to retrace Daddy's and my footsteps on our daily 6 P.M. walks, to place flowers on his grave, to stand in the knee-deep snow at the cemetery and to cry. And I cried, hard this time. I found myself repeating, "I have to let you go. I have to leave you here."

After this cleansing and closure, for the first time, I could talk about Dad without getting that mysterious lump in my throat. Gradually, I began to feel in control of my life. The ticking time bomb had been defused safely.

The primary goal of any of the strategies I have discussed is to enable you to match your emotions with the insights you acquire. Both are important. Any of these tactics can help dislodge repressed feelings. But they also can become just another intellectual exercise. If this happens, seek a therapist.

Some Words of Advice

Here is a thumbnail sketch of my advice to those of you who suffer from father hunger due to any of the seven sources discussed in chapter 4.

1. **If your father is dead and you are still grieved,** plan a ritual to "rebury" him. Only this time, do it being totally emotionally present, rather than merely getting through an ordeal. That is, bring your emotions to your intellectual understandings about his death. "Talk" to him. Tell him what you miss or have missed. Bring him flowers. Conduct your own memorial service. And then say "good-bye" literally.

2. **If your parents are divorced and you seldom or never see your father,** look him up. Treat his absence as adopted children must who truly wish to move on. Search for your father. If you know where he is, and still seldom if ever see him, initiate regular contact. This could be as innocuous as taking him out for breakfast once a month, or as momentous as a family-of-origin meeting to discuss the divorce and to finish it (emotionally, that is).

3. **If you were born to a single mother and scarcely or never knew your father,** get as much information from your mother as you possibly can about what she knew about your birth father. If you decide to look him up, plan carefully so you maximize the chances of a positive

outcome. You, too, will need to treat your situation as adopted children do who search for their birth parents do. Be sensitive to the fact that the people in his current life may know nothing of your existence, so a sudden, unplanned appearance will be a shock and probably will feel like an intrusion. And if you know who and where your birth father is but your contact is sporadic, initiate regular contact. Do ordinary activities like working on his car with him or going out for coffee. Just being with him will teach you about yourself while it helps you fill in some cracks. And if you had the unfortunate circumstance of having a sperm-donor father, you perhaps have the biggest challenge of all because you got the smallest scintilla of fatherhood there is. Your only recourse is to thank your mother for giving you life and talk to her to gain an understanding of what went into her decision to conceive you this way. And grieve—for all the voids in your life and in your psyche, for all that you simply will not know or experience.

4. **If you were adopted,** search for your father. Too often, adoptees search only for their birth mother, almost as if they were born by immaculate conception. Learning information about your father also is learning about yourself. At the very least, some day, it could be important to know your medical and genetic history.

5. **If your father was an active addict,** grieve the father you lost by his choosing drugs over you. Put the responsibility for that choice where it belongs: on him, not you.

6. **If your father abused you,** although it probably still will be terrifying, it is important that you set the record

straight directly with him. Countless times, I have sat with abusive fathers and their adult children as they hashed out earlier events. Almost invariably, these dads confess that they can see now that what they did was abuse. But that was how they were parented, so they thought that was how parenting should be done. It probably will take all the courage you can muster and many months of preparation, but until you take your issues up at the source, you will remain deep inside a scared little child who is susceptible to abuse by others.

7. **If you had or have a traditional father,** you may be confused about how you can feel a loss when he lived in the home with you. But you can. The loss is due to his lack of emotional availability. It may be helpful to remember many readers or their fathers grew up in an era with Ward and June Cleaver from *Leave It to Beaver* as role models. That means "good fathers" of that day were providers and disciplinarians. So it was simply not in a father's job description to be emotionally available. Here the definitions of "good father" and "adequate man" are severely at odds.

A Postscript About Veronica

Shortly after Veronica wrote the epistle to her parents contained in the beginning of this chapter, I went on a month-long summer vacation. When Veronica called me for an appointment upon my return, I expected an update on the fallout from her letter. Instead, I was surprised to learn that she had not sent it. She had it stamped and ready to mail when she received a call from a family member telling her of small strokes that her father had. Then, as she was pondering what to do, her mother called and told her of a month-long fight the parents had about a trivial matter. This clinched Veronica's thinking. She would not mail the letter. The risks outweighed the benefits. Besides, she no longer felt she needed to do so. She detailed the thinking that went into her decision.

> **Veronica:** I don't think they're up to the psychological and emotional task of being responsible parents, which is what I'd be asking them to do. It's too late. When my father dies, my mother and I will have a completely different relationship. I'll hang on to the letter and maybe give it to her then. It's sad because I don't have a relationship with him now and I guess I never will. I finally had the courage to try. But, at this point, it would do more harm than good. And my dad is really to be pitied now. He's always been, but he really is now. And anyway, I really feel some closure.
> **Beth:** How do you know?
> **Veronica:** Because I have more energy for other things.
> **Beth:** So the act of your writing the letter, plus your willingness to send it, makes actually sending it moot.
> **Veronica:** Yes. I just don't think that's the place I need to focus anymore.

It would surprise no one for me to say that at first I was suspicious that Veronica's choice was just another form of resistance. But as she talked, the words and the music were congruent, so I concluded it would have been a mistake to press the issue. She had a peace about her that I concluded I mustn't disturb.

No one needs to languish in the purgatory of unresolved father loss. Even if a father stonewalls and refuses to cooperate, that loss still can be and needs to be resolved. Doing so, in some ways, will be more arduous and, in many ways, less fulfilling than is restructuring a relationship with a cooperative father. However, it needs to be done. Otherwise, unexpressed sadness will color the world and will make genuine intimacy with anyone very difficult indeed.

References

1. Rusty Berkus, *To Heal Again: Towards Serenity and the Resolution of Grief* (Encino, Calif.: Red Rose Press, 1984), 6–7.

2. David Viscott, *Emotional Resilience: Simple Truths for Dealing with the Unfinished Business of Your Past* (New York: Random House Audiobooks, 1996).

3. C. B. Truax and Robert Carkoff, *Effective Counseling and Psychotherapy* (Chicago: Aldine, 1967), 21.

4. Elana Golomb, *Trapped in the Mirror: Adult Children of Narcissists in Their Struggle for Self* (New York: William Morrow, 1992), 53.

5. Ibid., 152.

9 Both Fathers and Mothers Are Important

> *Our mother gives us our earliest lessons*
> *in love—and its partner, hate.*
> *Our father—our "second other"*
> *—elaborates on them.*
>
> —Judith Viorst
> *Necessary Losses*

The answer to the question of whether fathers are more important than mothers is, in a word, no. Definitely not! Neither parent is more important in the life of a child. "And yet, in answering the question 'Does every child deserve a father?' our [society's] current answer hovers between 'no' and 'not necessarily.' "[1] Says psychiatrist Frank Pittman, "One of the first things that happened when we overthrew patriarchy two hundred years ago was the notion that women could raise children alone."[2] However, children need strong and stable attachments to both parents in order to make their way successfully in an increasingly complex world.

Fathers and mothers are not identical or interchangeable parts. With their reciprocal roles, *each* offers the child unique elements that contribute to its intellectual, psychological and social development. *Both* parents together and separately provide the supplies that are vital ingredients required for building a positive self-image for children and for helping them figure out how to constructively participate in society. And unfortunately, the preponderance of both psychological and sociological research indicates that no surrogate father can make up for the birth father's absence. For example, children of stepfamilies do no better than children of mothers who never remarry. Children in stepfamilies, particularly girls, leave their households earlier than do children in single-parent households or in two-parent households.[3]

In addition, a major reason for the increase in child abuse is that unrelated men, surrogate fathers, are more likely than natural fathers to abuse these children, probably because of the absence of early parent-child bonding between unrelated men and their stepchildren. And especially in single-parent families and stepfamilies, such men have more access to these children than ever before.[4] Therefore, strong attachment and bonding between father and child in infancy may be a critical ingredient for preventing later child abuse. Children who do not have a close and continuing relationship with their biological father are less likely than other children to have such a relationship with any adult male.[5] Thus, fatherlessness and father loss increasingly will become a transgenerational phenomenon that both results from and creates family dysfunction. So, however unconsciously, eventually a father's absence (for most children) becomes like the sky: it covers everything. And it is a stormy sky if his absence is volitional.

Furthermore, to a child, parents together and separately stand for safety. Therefore, fear of losing one or both parents is the earliest terror a child knows. And having this nightmare actually come true for a child is like surgery done with no anesthetic.

However, while the mother/child bond remains for most children the closest they have to an unbreakable bond, alas, it is not so with the father/child bond for all too many. The epidemic of fatherlessness is fast becoming a defining feature of the American childhood and family. As I have stated, the rise of volitional fatherlessness is creating a new definition of haves and have-nots.

As biological fatherhood is increasingly being separated from social and emotional fatherhood, children are left with two basic choices. Either they are consigned to pine away for him, feeling poignantly their unrequited love, or they must wall off both his absence and their need for him. Moreover, when walling off this significant a person, especially if it is early in their development, people unwittingly wall themselves in, and eventually a film of ice forms over their heart. So whichever choice children make, the father's absence becomes the defining characteristic of those children's lives, providing the color and texture for its entire tapestry. Thus, it is a father's absence that sometimes makes it seem as though he is more important than Mother. His significance is skewed by his absence. His leaving usually becomes a life-defining moment for those who are fortunate enough to have a recollection of it.

It has been said that mothers are born, fathers are made. And to the extent that is true, and as our society increasingly views fathers as disposable and even superfluous, more and more fathers are accepting that cultural norm and opting out of the chance to be molded and shaped into the role. Yet, being an active father is one powerful way men can fill the void created by their own father's emotional or literal absence. President Clinton, whose own father died before he was born and whose stepfather was abusive, has perhaps found a way to reparent himself by taking an active and committed role in parenting his daughter, Chelsea. One can speculate about how his father's absence may influence his behavior toward women, for better or worse.

Says Blankenhorn in his final chapter of *Fatherless America*:

> The most urgent domestic challenge facing the United States at the close of the twentieth century is the recreation of fatherhood as a vital social role for men. At stake is nothing less than the success of the American experiment. . . . To tolerate the trend of fatherlessness is to accept the inevitability of continued societal recession.[6]

Some believe that fatherlessness has already begun to change the shape and nature of our society. And if it continues, there is little reason to believe that we all will not begin to pay dearly. In fact, a plethora of statistics tell us that it is already costing individuals and our society dearly. A study conducted by researchers at Fordham University and cited in the *New York Times* reported that, "The nation's social well-being has fallen to its lowest point in almost twenty-five years, and children and young people are suffering the most."[7] Of course, children are the ones who can least afford to pay the price that is extracted by this societal trend. Although the newspaper article about the study reported no attempt by the researchers to define root causes, surely fatherlessness is a prime candidate. As we have seen, the increasingly fragmented experience with fatherhood that many children have leaves them with a hole in their soul that they can't begin to fill even with basic information, let alone daily contact and knowledge of him.

Severe separations in childhood from *either* parent leave emotional scars because they assault essential connections: those with our parents. Premature separations and interruptions in children's bonds to either parent skew their expectations of and responses to life. This dysfunction in turn creates more dysfunction, as the children of these families go on to form their own families. But when they have secure attachments to both parents, paradoxically they then can afford to let them go. Using the psychic supplies provided by these central relationships, they develop a positive self-image, a sturdy self-esteem that allows them genuinely to love themselves. Then they possess a love of self that sets them free to love others.

References

1. David Blankenhorn, *Fatherless America: Confronting Our Most Urgent Social Problem* (New York: Basic Books, 1995), 222.

2. Frank Pittman, "Father Hunger, Father Loss, Mothers Lose?" (Family Law Institute, New Mexico State Bar Association spring conference, 10 May 1996).

3. David Popenoe, *Life Without Father* (New York: Free Press, 1996), 9.

4. Ibid., 65.

5. Ibid., 140.

6. Blankenhorn, *Fatherless America*, 222.

7. Nick Ravo, "Index of Social Well-Being Is at the Lowest in Twenty-Five Years," *New York Times*, 14 October 1996, sec. A12.

Appendix A: What You Can and Can't Do for Someone Who Is Suffering

We cannot live, sorrow or die for
somebody else, for suffering is
too precious to be shared.

—Edward Dahlberg
Because I Was Flesh

Despite the controversy regarding exactly how divorce statistics are gathered, it is clear that the divorce rate is high among Americans. More and more people are beginning to consider what can be done to stem the tide. Many states are passing legislation intended to help (some say force) couples to stay married. A handful of states have legislated premarital counseling, and more legislatures are considering following suit. One state, Louisiana, is testing the belief that government can alter the rate at which marriages end by altering the way they begin. It offers licenses for two types of marriages, regular and covenant, with the latter being much harder to end.

As we have seen, absent and unavailable fathers hamper their children's development in several key ways. One is the assault on children's self-esteem that is committed by a father who opts out. Though not impossible, it is difficult for those children to develop the sturdy sense of self that is required to relate to another in a truly intimate manner. These children also are limited in their ability to observe a loving, working relationship between both parents that would serve as an internal blueprint for how intimate relationships are maintained.

One view on the reasons for contemporary high divorce rates is that unknown and unaddressed father loss becomes a prime barrier to marital intimacy. If this is the case, father loss can be seen as a core issue impacting couple functioning. Thus, it is important that this issue be addressed if it is a factor for couples to have the greatest chance for building a healthy connection characterized by relationship-enhancing dynamics.

While people contemplating marriage will be unable to resolve a potential spouse's father loss for the other person, they need to have their eyes open about its effects if it remains unresolved. Otherwise, they enhance the chances of becoming a statistic. And if this is important for a first marriage, it is essential for a second marriage because those statistics are particularly alarming. The divorce rate among those who married again in the 1980s so far is about 25 percent higher than it is for those who entered first marriages.[1] Thus, it is easy to see that being deliberate is particularly important when couples contemplate another marriage, so that they can attempt to ensure that they do not repeat their mistakes and jeopardize themselves and yet another family. And if my repeatedly stated contention is correct—that unresolved losses of all kinds have a singular capacity to jeopardize intimate relationships—then resolving them can be an important kind of inoculation against divorce.

This short chapter's primary purpose is to clarify what people can and cannot do for and with their loved ones who are chronically grieved about their father's absence. Its focus is on highlighting the potential risks for those contemplating marrying or committing to someone with unresolved father loss. Offering a list of *dos* and *don'ts*, I discuss the concerns for someone contemplating marrying a partner whom they suspect has unresolved father loss. I follow this by considerations for those already married to a spouse with these issues.

Premarital *Dos* and *Don'ts*

Dos for those considering marriage:

- **Do** look at what is in it for you to contemplate attaching yourself to someone with so central an issue as unresolved father loss.

- **Do** examine carefully your potential partner's willingness to face himself or herself. Those unwilling or unable to deal with themselves won't want to face you, either. This, obviously, will have an impact on the degree and quality of intimacy that you can achieve in your marriage.

- **Do** ask yourself what attracted you to an emotionally unavailable partner. Is this a familiar role for you because of your relationship with your own father?

- **Do** gauge carefully the basis of your attraction to this person. If it is having someone who's a perpetual "fixer-upper," both of you will grow weary of and feel constrained by that burden.

- **Do** be sure you are dealing with your own issues. Sometimes people mate with those with a broken wing so they themselves don't have to learn how to fly.

- **Do** be sure that the nature of your attraction to this person is not based in your need to be a caretaker.

- **Do** become and remain aware of how both people's issues interact; this will help you take responsibility for your contribution to the problems in your relationship and not blame your partner for everything. In shifting blame, you give away your influence to change the situation, while you wait for the benevolence, insight and motivation of your partner to prompt the necessary changes.

- **Do** seek premarital counseling if you have children, are a child of divorce, have been divorced or are unsure of how to assess and address any of the comments in this list.

Don'ts for those considering marriage:

- **Don't** expect your partner to make up for all the parenting you didn't get. It is normal to get some childhood emotional cracks filled in by a spouse, but it is dangerous to expect it or demand it.

- **Don't** buy into your partner's hope, expectation or fantasy that you can fill all his or her voids, either.

- **Don't** marry so you can be the savior. If your partner gets healthy and works you out of a job, you will have lost the basis of the relationship. Besides, what would give your life meaning then?

- **Don't** marry to rescue or to be rescued.

- **Don't** marry someone who refuses to deal with his or her issues or with you.

- **Don't** marry someone expecting that she or he will change. People do change each other in the course of their life together, but when your partner's changing is the price of admission to your heart, you only invite perpetual power struggles and eventual exhaustion and disillusionment.

For Those Already Married

Those already married when unresolved father loss comes to light have a different set of considerations, particularly if they have children. Mostly those have to do with making sure who owns the problem and how the loss is resolved. Those who are confused about that become classic enablers and codependents.

Dos for those married to a chronically grieved spouse:

- **Do** have a healthy respect for how frightening examining deep and painful issues and renegotiating for a different kind of relationship with fathers is—for both of you. This, in turn, will require that the spouses shift their relationship. This is usually frightening, no matter how necessary.

- **Do** be empathic and supportive, unless your spouse likes being a victim or staying stuck. Then take a "tough love" stance. But do so deliberately and lovingly, not vengefully.

- **Do** remember that this is not your issue to resolve.

- **Do** remember that you chose this person. Be sure you figure out why and how healthy those reasons were. If you determine that they were not as laudable as you thought, instead of throwing out the baby with the bath water, attempt to work on restructuring the marriage. You would be well advised to do this with a marital therapist so you minimize the chances of becoming a divorce statistic.

- **Do** see a trained marital therapist if you suspect that your marriage or your reasons for being in it aren't healthy. That person can help the two of you develop a new marital contract.

- **Do** remember that the poor parenting a spouse received is not his or her fault. Don't blame your spouse for it or allow it to be used as an excuse.

- **Do** be patient.

Don'ts for those married to a chronically grieved spouse:

- **Don't** take on your spouse's problem or feelings. This will leave you resentful and your spouse's loss still unresolved.

- **Don't** blame your spouse for the current state of affairs. However, this is not the same as holding him or her accountable. Mutual accountability is a major ingredient of successful relationships.

- **Don't** expect miracles overnight.

- **Don't** be patient to a fault, either, if your spouse is hiding behind his or her troubled childhood. Then, rather than being supportive, you'll be a chump.

- **Don't** be afraid to examine your options if your spouse refuses to cooperate and heal. Even if you stay in the relationship, there will be a much firmer commitment because of your having honestly and courageously considered whether or not you truly want and need to stay.

References

1. Bryan Strong and Christine DeVault, *The Marriage and Family Experience,* 5th ed. (St. Paul: West Publishing, 1992), 517.

READER/CUSTOMER CARE SURVEY

If you are enjoying this book, please help us serve you better and meet your changing needs by taking a few minutes to complete this survey. Please fold it & drop it in the mail.

Name: _____

Address: _____

_____

Tel. # _____

(1) Gender: 1) ____ Female 2) ____ Male

(2) Age: 1)____ 18-25 4)____ 46-55
2)____ 26-35 5)____ 56-65
3)____ 36-45 6)____ 65+

(3) Marital status:

1)____ Married 3)____ Single 5)____ Widowed
2)____ Divorced 4)____ Partner

(4) Is this book: 1) ____ Purchased for self?
2)____ Purchased for others?
3)____ Received as gift?

(5) How did you find out about this book?

1)____ Catalog 2)____ Store Display
Newspaper
3)____ Best Seller List
4)____ Article/Book Review
5)____ Advertisement
Magazine
6)____ Feature Article
7)____ Book Review
8)____ Advertisement
9)____ Word of Mouth
A)____ T.V./Talk Show (Specify) _____
B)____ Radio/Talk Show (Specify) _____
C)____ Professional Referral _____
D)____ Other (Specify) _____

Which Health Communications book are you currently reading?

As a special **"Thank You"** we'll send you exciting news about interesting books and a valuable Gift Certificate.
It's Our Pleasure to Serve You!

(6) What subject areas do you enjoy reading most? (Rank in order of enjoyment)

1)____ Women's Issues/   5)____ New Age/
Relationships   Altern. Healing
2)____ Business Self Help 6)____ Aging
3)____ Soul/Spirituality/ 7)____ Parenting
Inspiration   8)____ Diet/Nutrition/
4)____ Recovery   Exercise/Health

(14) What do you look for when choosing a personal growth book?

(Rank in order of importance)
1)____ Subject   3)____ Author
2)____ Title   4)____ Price
Cover Design 5)____ In Store Location

(19) When do you buy books?

(Rank in order of importance)
1)____ Christmas
2)____ Valentine's Day
3)____ Birthday
4)____ Mother's Day
5)____ Other (Specify _____

(23) Where do you buy your books?

(Rank in order of frequency of purchases)
1)____ Bookstore   6)____ Gift Store
2)____ Price Club   7)____ Book Club
3)____ Department Store 8)____ Mail Order
4)____ Supermarket/   9)____ T.V. Shopping
Drug Store   A)____ Airport
5)____ Health Food Store

Additional comments you would like to make to help us serve you better.

_____

_____

Thank You !!

FOLD HERE

BUSINESS REPLY MAIL
FIRST CLASS MAIL PERMIT NO 45 DEERFIELD BEACH, FL

POSTAGE WILL BE PAID BY ADDRESSEE

HEALTH COMMUNICATIONS
3201 SW 15TH STREET
DEERFIELD BEACH, FL 33442-9875

Appendix B:
How Therapists Can Help

All therapists can tell stories: about their favorite clients; about their toughest case, about the case on which they totally missed the boat; about the biggest mystery they had to solve. As a practicing family psychologist for over twenty years, I have my share of stories in each of these categories. One that stands out, even after fifteen years, is the story of Karla and Marty.

Karla's psychiatrist was unsuccessful in controlling her depression with drug therapy. Because he wished to avoid hospitalizing her, he referred her to me. She had become significantly more depressed, but he was unable to pinpoint why and was concerned about the risk of suicide.

Assuming her depression was her problem, she protectively balked when I gently insisted that her husband, Marty, would need to join us. But she was desperate to get relief from "the blackness." So she agreed to ask Marty to join us, even though she was puzzled about how and why.

Karla, twenty-six, was a homemaker and mother of three children. Marty, an enlisted man in the armed services, showed up in his full dress uniform. He also was twenty-six years old. They were high school sweethearts who hurriedly married when they thought Karla was pregnant. Discovering after the marriage that she was not, she did become pregnant a short time later.

To get comfortable with each other, I began by asking both of them my two customary questions: "What brings you here? How do you hope I can help?" Tears immediately streamed from Karla. "I'm depressed, and Marty wants a divorce." First, I validated her sadness and depression, saying it seemed like a reasonable response to such a pronouncement. Then, I turned to Marty and asked whether that was accurate, and what he understood about why. He nodded, stating flatly, "I don't know why. I just do." He seemed genuinely chagrined, unable to put his finger on why; he just wanted out. They had been married for seven years.

Then I asked another customary question: "What brings you to therapy now?" At that, Karla began to describe her panic when Marty had been sent to school by the military for six weeks. Because the school was located several states away and they lived on a tight budget, both his coming home and her visiting him were impossible. Even phone calls had to be infrequent and frustratingly brief. In the few weeks since Marty's return, Karla found herself vacillating between the extremes of raging and crying. At that point, Marty got a pained look on his face and said, "She's like a little girl, clutching at my ankles all the time!" His facial expression and tone of voice suggested that he clearly was repulsed, and Karla knew it. Still, she felt powerless to stop. By this time, Karla was crying profusely, and makeup-blackened tears streamed down her contorted face. Both were totally bewildered about why Marty wanted a divorce in the first place and about why Karla couldn't stop her infantile behavior.

At that moment, ten minutes into the first interview, I played my first hunch. "Karla, how old were you when your father died?" Her eyes snapped to attention, and she said, "Three! But I never saw him. My mother threw him out of the delivery room the day I was born, so I never laid eyes on him!" Because it was far too soon to work with that information, I paused for a minute to let it sink in for all of us, and mentally tagged it for future discussion. She seemed stunned enough and grateful that I did not explore her pain.

The conversation resumed without a great deal of focus. Usually, in the first interview, I prefer to learn about a couple's dynamics by going tourist to wherever they take me. Then Marty began talking about his family of origin. Making no mention of his father, he shared that he was the oldest of three children who had grown up in a low-income housing project in a small Southern city. His demeanor showed little animation, and his speech was flat, despite his Southern drawl. He punctuated this description by once again noting his bemusement about why he would want to leave Karla. So I tried my second hunch. "How old were you when your father left?" Shocked, he replied, "Seven! Now how did you know all that?" I felt like Archimedes. Eureka! Thirty minutes into the first interview, I already had the keys to two core issues that underlay their current relationship impasse and their personal styles.

Karla, already abandoned by her father by the time she saw the light of day, reacted violently to any further hint of abandonment. This was manifest in her alternating between the extremes of neediness and clinging, and fury and threatening. Each was to ward off fears. By contrast, Marty had developed a personal style characterized by detachment. The more needy and threatened he felt, the more detached he became. Because when people feel threatened, they usually revert to their most primitive response, Marty cloaked his fear at being isolated and away from home by withdrawing and detaching. I surmised that he had developed this style from his very limited experience with feeling attached to anyone. When his father abandoned the family, his mother became understandably preoccupied with work so that she could provide for her family and keep it together. So, in effect, she disappeared at the same time. Marty spent the majority of his life after that alone, isolating himself even from his siblings. Thus, he had no clue about how to connect in an intimate way. This was the basis of his anxiety when Karla, out of her anxiety at his detachment, became smothering in her neediness. Her begging for reassurance from him generated virtually an allergic reaction in Marty. So he would take more distance. Which made her all the more clingy. By the time they began couples therapy, anger had become their only pathway "safe" for connecting. However, this, too, would stir up Karla's fear of abandonment, which stirred up Marty's fear of being smothered. So they were exhausted cats chasing their tails, each needing a kind of reassurance that the other could not give.

Piecing Together Clues to
Karla and Marty's Case

Good therapists are good detectives, piecing together clues, bits and pieces of evidence that solve the mystery of the misery that people bring to us for our help. What clues helped me piece Karla and Marty's case together?

Usually, the presentation made by the client provides the initial tip. Karla's excessive panic at the possibility of being left was the first suggestion that something in her past was reverberating in the current crisis. Although Marty's pronouncement surely was alarming, Karla's reaction seemed grossly out of proportion. Since she obviously had been helpless at birth about her father's abandoning her, I hypothesized that the threat of Marty's leaving set off reverberations of her imprint experience of being helpless when abandoned by her father, compounded by Marty's gross indifference to her pain. As she talked, I even got a mental image of her as an infant clutching Marty's ankles while he tried to get away. Although she obviously was enraged at Marty for self-evident reasons, I surmised that she was enraged at her own impotence as well. Although, of course, the threat of being divorced against her will would naturally be depressing, "the blackness" began when Marty left for school. Depression, particularly if it is chronic and catalyzed by no apparent cause, always prompts me to assess for chronic, unresolved loss.

In contrast to Karla's effusiveness, Marty's flatness and detachment were his primary initial clues. I suspected that his extreme aloofness was not just situational, but rather was a manifestation of a chronic state for him. His coldness got me wondering about emotional as well as economic deprivation in his childhood. Which got me speculating—who had summarily and suddenly detached from him, as he now proposed to do from his family? Referred to as repetition compulsion in the psychoanalytic literature, people's unconscious drive to repeat their earliest scenarios is powerful indeed. One reason is because it is familiar, it is "normal," and therefore, individuals' need for homeostasis is satisfied. Because of their sense of profound familiarity, they know their lines and moves. Another, more healthy urge is to attempt this time to master their situation. Whatever the source, Marty's indifference and detachment defended him well. Nobody could get to him to cause him to feel abandoned ever again. In fact, he had found a way to protect himself by feeling nothing. Period!

Another indicator that seemed to point to childhood traumas was the sevens. For reasons that are their own mystery, unconscious reminders of traumatic earlier events begin to reverberate when a current event involves that same number. For example, Marty was seven years old at the time his father left. Their older daughter was seven. The couple had been married for seven years. This pointed in the direction of a trauma for Marty at age seven. So I played my hunch and hit the jackpot again.

However, probably the single most powerful data base I had that made me attuned to such trauma for these clients was my own countertransferences from my childhood experiences.

Diagnostic Issues Specific to Father Loss

The two central, specific diagnostic questions are: Is loss at the heart of the presenting problem? If so, how has this loss affected the client's present relationship functioning?

In the mind of both therapist and client, it can be a challenge to tie an event that happened so far in the past and has been so well hidden into a client's current dysfunction. All too often, it is tempting to take people at their word, focusing, for example, on their sexual dysfunction or on their fights, without considering the function these symptoms serve for the individual, couple or family. If father loss is the fuel for these symptoms and it is not drained, symptoms are likely to pop up elsewhere. Often, the symptoms with which clients present are acute exacerbations of unresolved grief, which is why, as in Karla and Marty's case, clients are not being coy or elusive when they say they do not know which repressed emotions and events triggered the exacerbation of their problem. Usually, however, it is messages embedded deeply in their unconscious or relationship dynamics they developed in response that make their current problem so compelling.

Formulating Hypotheses

When people begin telling their story, I begin to shape my formulation of their case by generating hypotheses. Most are idiosyncratic to the individuals I am interviewing, but some arise out of my general theory and philosophy of therapy. I have acknowledged a clearly stated bias that loss often is at the heart of the presenting problem. And sheer logic says that what is not identified accurately will not be treated. I thus begin testing to see whether or not my general hypothesis fits in this specific case. Of course, people are not compelled to have an unresolved loss in their history. If I find no evidence, I simply discard that conjecture—but not until I have checked carefully.

Since people with such an unresolved trauma have been keeping it out of sight and out of mind for virtually a lifetime, most are loath to have it uncovered. However, taking even a cursory history can help expose these losses. If I leave it up to people who have denied a significant event for a lifetime, I will wait a long time! Often, I need to hunt for the information required to form an initial diagnosis. In addition to their history, their here-and-now presentation week-to-week in my office also will contain some valuable clues.

A symptom is a symptom. The key issue is to find what the symptom is covering and treat what it masks. Doing so usually resolves the symptoms in the process. If it does not, by that stage in therapy, clients usually are amenable to learning the requisite new skills for relating better, because they feel safe enough to give up self-protection in the other's presence. Does this mean that symptom resolution is unimportant? Of course not! Therapists who pay no attention to this are not in business for long! But it does mean that if they get too caught up in the intricacy and the elegance of the symptom itself, they will not be helping in the long run. My experience tells me that the symptoms gradually begin to recede when the forces that propel them are eliminated.

Some Final Considerations About Diagnosis

To summarize, some considerations about the initial phase of treatment are:

1. Diagnosis and treatment are inseparable. That means, as soon as therapists begin testing their hypotheses with clients, they are making an intervention. Rather than seeing

these two concepts as wholly separate categories, it is more helpful and accurate to see both on a continuum. That is, one cannot do one without the other. For example, when I inquired about Karla's father's death, I, of course, was testing the hypothesis of the relationship between the loss occasioned by that death and her depression. But I also was making an intervention, because in highlighting that loss as a potential issue, I was beginning to craft a way to help them understand and change what previously had mystified them.

2. The corollary assumption to the previous one is that diagnosis is a continuing process, and is not finalized and beyond consideration again as soon as one decides on a DSM-IV diagnostic code. Diagnosis should be taking place before and after every intervention, in order to gauge client readiness, the intervention's effectiveness and the client's progression in the process of healing.

3. The first few times—or the first several times, with well-defended clients—that I propose that they experienced father loss, I often get either blank stares or flat-out denial. Often, when I persist, clients might allow that there is a loss, but most deny its significance or that it has any relevance now. So be prepared to persist gently when clients have given historical data, as Karla and Marty did, that would substantiate the diagnosis of unresolved father loss.

4. Have a healthy respect for the fact that, by now, denial has become a way of life for folks who experience chronic, unresolved father loss. So probe carefully, insist softly. Because by now denial is second nature and since

people have built their personality around it, it wouldn't be pretty if their denial came crashing down all at once.

5. If I have historical data to substantiate my diagnosis, a client's continued denial of the significance of a previous experience confirms my hypothesis, unless there are multiple indicators such as those listed in chapter 8 that tell me the trauma is resolved.

6. I generally do not treat father loss in the first phase of treatment, when I first identify it. And even when clients agree with my formulation, I work toward its treatment by laying groundwork that permits people to resolve the loss only as they become genuinely ready. That is, most people have repressed most or all feelings in order to keep so powerful an experience as loss out of sight and out of mind. So most need to be taught a new vocabulary and need to learn how to access their feelings in general. Also, if the grieved client is in a significant relationship that I assess has been damaged by one or both persons' defensiveness, then that dynamic and pattern need to be addressed before there will be enough trust between them to take on the father loss.

What Is a Source Experience?

From time to time, even the best, most seasoned therapists feel stuck. Often with recalcitrant clients and sometimes even the most motivated, both therapists and clients trip again and again over a subtle but keenly felt barrier to change. These are the vexing times when both therapists and clients feel like Sisyphus pushing the rock up the hill, only to have it roll back down again, each time generating an ordeal and diminishing hope for everyone involved.

This roadblock impedes clients' growth as well as progress in treatment, despite their sincere wish to the contrary. One way to understand the phenomenon is by using the concept of source experience. What initially may appear to be an elaborate game of stump-the-therapist probably is the intrusion of a relic from the client's past in the form of a source experience. This is the sort of experience that has left its indelible mark on the client and is the root of the present bottleneck. Sometimes the source experience is obvious, such as parents' decision to divorce. Sometimes it is subtler, such as the parents' announcement of their decision to divorce. In one client's case, his profound loss of his beloved mother when he was fourteen years old was traumatic to him. But the main fount of his distress, it turned out, was his traditional father's business-like handling of her death and of the children after the funeral. His mother died on a Friday, and when the family returned home from the funeral, my client reported that his father's only words were, "It's a good thing the funeral was on Friday, so this family will be back to normal by Monday." That was that. You easily can infer how crushing this statement was to the children as they buried their mother and lost their father on the same day. Imagine the multiple contortions they had to put themselves through to comply with the father's implied demand.

To change something responsibly, we first must know it in context. Little of substance can be changed if we fail to understand *how and why dysfunctional responses develop*. The primary source of fodder for behavior that clients themselves even know is irrational develops from events variously described: Robert and Mary Goulding referred to these events

as early decisions in 1979;[1] Janet Johnston and Linda Campbell called them nuclear family scripts in 1988;[2] and Norman
and Betty Paul referred to them as source experiences in 1986.[3]
Whatever they are called, these are the indelible images that
form a template for how individuals and families "should" be
and provide the "logic" for people's illogical, unconstructive
behavior. When you help clients identify these events, examine these motifs and discharge the emotional kindling they
encapsulate, the power of these experiences finally can be
diminished significantly, if not dissipated entirely.

How Do Therapists Structure Treatment with a Primary Goal to Resolve Father Loss?

I want to reiterate that treatment of any client on any issue
is not a one-size-fits-all proposition. So certainly it is not so
with an issue as idiosyncratically difficult as one based on an
early trauma like father loss. Therefore, there is much more to
generalize about regarding diagnosis than there is regarding
treatment.

Understanding Content and Process: Keys to Structuring Interventions

I propose a two-pronged approach, whatever specific strategy is selected, for choosing interventions for clients. One
prong is to facilitate the surfacing of clients' emotions. The
other is to combine this prong with new insights and understandings. Continuing cycles of experience (expressing their
emotions) plus reflecting on that experience (deriving cognitive
understandings or insights) is what is required for developmental growth and change, not mere learning.[4] Continuing this

looping throughout treatment is what eventually resolves the trauma and helps people change themselves, their symptoms and their systems along the way. Therefore, therapists need to be attuned to the difference between content and process.

A research finding twenty-five years ago by communications theorists is now so commonly accepted that it has passed into general understanding. That is the conclusion that only 7 percent of the meaning of a given communication is contained in the words; the real meaning is contained in the remaining 93 percent, which is composed of tone, voice, nonverbal cues, the timing of a statement and so on. If clients entertain the family and me at appropriate times with their dazzling sense of humor, I laugh and am charmed. But if they make a joke just after I have asked them about their divorce or adoption, I begin speculating. This is the difference between content and process. Unfortunately, too many therapeutic modalities seem either to be unaware of this difference, or they choose to ignore it. They do so with great risk. I have seen countless pictures of Michelangelo's *Pietà*, but they neither compared to nor prepared me for the awesome experience of seeing it for myself.

When process and content don't jibe, there will be confusion and even discord. It is the therapist's job to help clients learn to put the words and the music together. In my postdoctoral training, the father of another trainee died. After I extended my condolences, I asked my compatriot how he was doing. His response was, "Oh, I'm fine. I went out for an afternoon and took care of it." Clearly, the way he described his process belied the content of his words. Therapists not only can glean a great deal of information diagnostically from such statements, but also, if this man had been a client and not a colleague, his response would have told me where to point my initial interventions.

Making the distinction between content and process is simple and yet at the same time complex and subtle. It is so significant a construct that I rely on it to guide many of my therapeutic interventions. I also do a snippet of psycho-education about it with my clients. The purpose of making such a distinction is founded in the belief that relationship difficulties come out of people's polarized and unconscious defenses (their relational processes), not merely because of lack of communication skills and functional behavior (content). Of course, skill deficits become factors, too. But emphasizing them to the exclusion of the underlying processes allows us to be seduced by the belief that a problem so complex as those we are discussing can be fixed in easy steps by offering a few snappy techniques and emphasizing behavior change. As Herb Goldberg said when describing relationships, "Content is the seducer or the web that pulls others in. The process is the 'poison' that distorts and then destroys relationships."[5]

A Word of Caution

Therapeutic strategies not firmly rooted in solid theoretical grounding too often merely are a flash in the pan. When they don't work, you don't know why; and when they do work, you are pleased but equally mystified. Therefore, using any of these intervention strategies, but certainly the most complicated ones, requires theoretical footing. You have been given a basic look at developmental, psychodynamic and family systems theory throughout this book. In order to attain further competency in using these interventions, I urge you to delve into the works of the authors referenced throughout.

Therapeutic Interventions

With the multiple caveats just discussed, I offer the following treatment interventions. Surely, these are not the only or the best. They are, however, some of my favorites. Of course, any intervention needs to be selected and designed on a case-by-case, situation-by-situation basis as you tailor it to what you know of your clients and their needs at each phase of treatment. It is useful and appropriate to suggest journaling to most clients in the first session. But open-chair work that early would probably leave clients feeling denuded. An intervention attempted too soon, before clients are ready, probably will be responded to like yesterday's leftovers, or worse. But the same intervention attempted at another point along the way may facilitate a breakthrough. Therapists need to develop the wisdom of the diamond cutter, whose cut can either produce a gorgeous gem or a pile of carbon. This ability is known as clinical judgment, and it, perhaps more than any other capacity, separates the artists from the technicians.

Sample Strategies

In offering treatment strategies, I will divide my comments into two sections. The first deals with interventions that any reasonably well trained counselor or therapist could implement. The second section contains more complex interventions, for which additional training and reading would be advised. I have chosen to include strategies of the latter kind so that ambitious readers: can know a broader range of potential techniques that can be applied to this highly complex issue; and can be aware of the nature of additional training they need to put these complex arrows in their quiver.

None of these procedures is likely to resolve clients' loss in one fell swoop. Devise your own strategies with individualized knowledge of your client in mind, *as long as these interventions are grounded in theory*. Use my sample strategies to start your creative juices flowing. All of the suggestions, such as journaling or visiting the cemetery, that I made to lay readers in chapter 8, apply here. Always follow any exercise by processing it with clients, with the goal being to tease out new insights and to combine them with the emotions that accompany them.

Basic Treatment Strategies for Resolving Father Loss

Open-Chair Work

Description of the technique: Noted Gestalt therapist Fritz Perls employed this Gestalt technique. When I identify a "therapeutic moment," in order to minimize client's resistance, I ask how experimental he feels that day. If clients are willing to try the technique, as another way to minimize their resistance, I warn them that they probably will feel silly. But I want them to be themselves and talk to whoever or whatever I have "placed" in the chair I have just put opposite them. Then, when I intuit a natural break in their thinking or when I see a chance to heighten the affect, I ask them to change chairs, be X, and respond to [the client's name]. I continue in this manner until either I have accomplished what I was aiming for, until the client's resistance has worn out or until clients genuinely need a break.

Instructions for implementing the technique: A common cue that clients could gain from this technique is when they make statements like, "A part of me is furious that my dad worked so much, and a part of me understands the financial pressure he must have felt." I generally have one of four goals in mind. One is to help clients bring internal consistency to two (or more) warring parts of themselves in order to help them resolve their own conflicted feelings about a situation. A second goal is when they need to talk to their father to find out how they really feel because not talking about it keeps them stuck. A third is to get closure on an experience, and a fourth is to be able to get something off their chest. It is easy to get stuck defensively in the closed feedback loop in our heads and never find out what we really think or feel. This helps both to tune in to our inner dialogue and to resolve the clamor in our mind. Examples of times when such a technique might be helpful are when people need to be able to "talk" to their higher power or unavailable parent. In each of these conversations, the healthier parts of clients provide answers to the stuck part.

Creative Visualization

Description of the technique: Akin to open-chair work, clients relax and pay attention to their breathing, which puts them in a light trance. I use this strategy when people are having trouble remembering key events or anything much about their childhood. I ask people to pick a typical day in their life and imagine their being able to relive it. I invite them to remember everyday things like who woke them up in the morning, who was there after school, what color the walls were in their favorite bedroom and so on. The point is to give them access to information that they can "see" as it happened, rather than editing it through their conscious mind. This is a good strategy to use when people seem stuck. Sometimes, they are unable to access emotional or repressed information because they can't stop intellectualizing. This bypasses their conscious control. Sometimes, like open-chair work, I suggest this strategy to help people put a different and better ending on an event they remember. Other times, I use this technique early in treatment with people who are too inhibited to do open-chair work. Willing clients can be helped to visualize anything the therapist ethically would deem necessary at the time.

Instructions for implementing the technique: Simply suggest that people find a comfortable spot in their chair that they can hold for a while. Then invite them to close their eyes if they wish. And then, merely be the narrator or tour guide on whatever journey you want them to take. Speak slowly and softly. Do not include specific information in your narration, such as saying that their room was on the second floor or the house was white. If you guess wrong or become prescriptive, they will spend the rest of the time mentally fighting the process. Remember that emotions often are embedded in small, everyday details. So asking to see their favorite toy or where their parent's room was located relative to theirs will help them revivify what you are hoping to help them access. *You are not asking them to remember, because that will re-engage their conscious mind. Rather, you are asking them to see.*

Rituals

Description of the technique: Readers who are interested in learning more about this technique are urged to read *Rituals in Our Times* by Evan Imber-Black and Janine Roberts.[6] This very practical volume will provide a detailed discussion of the theory underlying this technique, as well as a thorough discussion of its implementation. However, because of its usefulness for a host of applications, a brief discussion is indicated for our purposes here. Rituals are powerful culminating events, as I experienced with the ritual I did for my dad. They help people finally, in essence, put the period at the end of a sentence. All societies throughout time have devised their own rituals. These practices have several advantages. Perhaps the most significant in this context is that rituals help people mark beginnings and ends. This is especially powerful when people are finally ready to let go. I have suggested a ritual when a client's own divorce or that of a parent has been only a legal one and not an emotional one. Or I use it when people have been unable, for one reason or another, to attend a funeral. I also use it when people have been able to unearth any information whatsoever about their adoptive father but they need to and are ready to accept the final loss. The uses are limited only by the creativity of the client and the therapist. Sometimes, these rituals are done in session, such as burning haunting memorabilia together. Sometimes, they are done out of session, such as finally sprinkling a dead loved one's ashes in the favorite place of the deceased or burying painful mementos in an appropriate spot.

Instructions for implementing the technique: Although rituals can be done to mark minilosses that are embedded in the overall father loss, I usually save them as a crescendo. They can be very useful to allow people to experience finality, so I caution therapists against suggesting this technique prematurely or if clients are not ready to let go. Otherwise, the experience will seem like cold oatmeal. When I sense that clients are ready, I begin by offering a brief description of the function of rituals, much as I did in the earlier paragraph. I suggest that clients think about what they might do between sessions and that we talk about it together next time. Underscoring that I am merely brainstorming, I offer descriptions of rituals that either I myself have participated in or that clients have done and then reported on, in order to prime the pump. However, I leave it up to clients to design and carry out their ritual, unless they specifically request my participation, as did one client who was too young to grasp the meaning of his father's death when he died. So he decided to "rebury" him. He contacted his rabbi and asked to use the temple, invited a few of his close friends, conducted a memorial service at the synagogue, burned some nonessential mementos, and scattered these ashes over his favorite place. Finally, he invited this group of supporters back to his home to sit shivah with him. The relief and closure he experienced were virtually palpable when he came to the next session.

Advanced Treatment Strategies

Hypnosis

Description of the technique: Hypnosis is one of the two "surgical" techniques at a highly trained therapist's disposal. The other is the family-of-origin session, which will be described. The power of hypnosis is that it acts like a laser beam in its precision, allowing willing subjects to bypass the censoring of their conscious mind. That is, it allows people to put their focus precisely where it needs to be to accomplish the treatment goal. This powerful tool is useful in the context of the resolution of loss in two primary ways. One is that, like visualization, it helps people "see" events that they cannot otherwise consciously retrieve. The other use is that it can be very helpful to close a chronically open chapter. I once treated a client whose psychiatrist referred her for "talk therapy" when his chemical interventions did no good. Our client still had nightmares for years, so when she finally came to my office, she looked as ragged as a concentration camp detainee. After many months and both of us prowling around trying to find out where she was stuck yielded no relief, I hit upon the idea of revisiting her father's funeral using hypnosis. We had worked with his death, which occurred when my client was sixteen years old, and with his molesting her from the time she was eight years old with his rough, laborer's hands, despite her begging him to stop. Still, all the tears shed and insights gained did not stop her nightmares. In the meantime, she was becoming more and more ragged and unable to function.

With her full knowledge and consent, I induced a trance and asked her to get a picture of her father's funeral. As she described the events that day, she gasped and almost bolted up out of her trance. When I asked her what she was seeing, she described how she had stomped out of the funeral in the middle and did not come back. However, until that minute, she had forgotten this. Clue number one: She had refused to participate in the first part of the community ritual that would have given her closure. After she stomped out, she sat in the car that would take her to the cemetery but refused to get out and go to the graveside. Although she logically knew that he was dead and buried, she did not know with emotional certainty. Her nightmares began that night and continued every night since. Finally grasping what the problem was, I took her through steps that would recapitulate the experience from which she had opted out. At the time she left the funeral, she had decided that it finally was safe to rebel against her father and that doing so was most important. Although I agreed that finally shucking off his authority was important, she inadvertently had created a situation ripe for chronic lack of closure. I asked her under hypnosis if she could see me going with her and could see herself getting out of the car. She agreed and did so. Then, I suggested that we step over to the casket. This was so terrifying for her that it took some minutes before she indicated that she had. And then she gasped. When I asked her what she saw then, she shrieked, "It's open! The casket's open!" Finally we had found the problem. In her mind, her father could still prowl around and abuse her by haunting her dreams. So if she refused to sleep, she couldn't dream and he'd have no control of her. Paradoxically, of course, her inability to resolve her grief for his life with her and his death also meant he had control, but she didn't realize that yet. Quietly, I suggested that she simply see herself closing the lid. Her trepidation was obvious as she saw herself approaching the casket, but she managed to do so. Then she triumphantly said: "I heard the click! It's shut now." That intervention was so powerful that this client reported to the following session bursting with enthusiasm. She had slept the night of the last session and every night since.

A note of caution: I am acutely aware of the controversy regarding the use of hypnosis as it relates to false-memory syndrome. A hypnotic subject is highly suggestible, eager to please and impatient to feel better. For these reasons, this technique must be used with caution, and the reliability of the results must be examined carefully and not automatically taken at face value. It is easy for the unethical hypnotherapist to lead a hypnotic subject into communicating with plants or animals, clucking like chickens, or believing the therapist's agenda. When this happens, the therapist's actions are dangerous to the client, can exacerbate the mental condition the therapist is attempting to heal and are flatly unethical practice.

To guard against the implantation of false memories, the therapist's questions must be very general. For example, the savvy reader will note that my primary question to my client was, "What do you see?" I did not ask her, "What did your father do to you?" This would have been more prescriptive than descriptive. Many therapists believe it is difficult not to be directive to a person under hypnosis. And in fact, I did become prescriptive in leading my client to close her father's coffin, for therapeutic purposes. This technique proved to be effective in this instance. However, others may have employed other techniques with as satisfactory an outcome. Careful training and supervised experience are essential to properly carrying out such a sophisticated, powerful and potentially dangerous technique.

Family-of-Origin Work: Coaching

Description of the technique: A central concept of the psychodynamic approach of Murray Bowen, one of the founders of the field of family therapy, is to stress the importance of understanding the contribution of people's family of origin to their current problem.[7] Bowen was so committed to this concept that the sole curriculum of his psychiatric residents for the bulk of their two-year rotation was to understand their own family of origin. Although others, such as James Framo,[8] another founder of our field, conducted actual family-of-origin sessions similar to those described in the next section, Bowen coached his clients to return home to hold these discussions. Bowen's goal was to help each person form a one-to-one adult relationship with every member of the family.

The role of the therapist as coach is simply to prepare clients to have an open and frank conversation with their father. Included in the preparation is strategizing for the potential reactions people could have, as well as for the inevitable age regression that happens when clients try to become adults in their own and their parents' eyes. The point is to help clients figure out how to go home and be an adult in everyone's eyes, rather than still be their parents' child.

Although Bowen did not emphasize the expression and resolution of emotions, and he decried emotions as reactivity to be avoided, my innovation on his approach is to work toward helping clients prepare to insert their previously unexpressed emotions into these discussions. Doing so has the greatest promise of bearing the fruit of new and potentially life-changing understandings.

A note of caution: Do not send home a lamb to the slaughter. If clients, for one good reason or another, cannot bring in the family to be seen by me, it is important to assess carefully, even if by proxy, how receptive key family members are likely to be to a solo conversation. If I have repeatedly gotten the sense that these key players are too narcissistic or rigid or abusive to hear and respond constructively, I suggest that this conversation take place in my office. For some clients, I don't suggest either type of direct conversation. In deciding on the best approach, I have learned to take many of my clients' descriptions of family members with a grain of salt. A key diagnostic issue is to discern whether their reported view of their family is merely their resistance, their anachronistic, childlike view talking, or whether they have a legitimate concern based in reality.

Family-of-Origin Work: Extended Family Session

Description of the technique: Although the goal is the same as with coaching, the methodology is markedly different. This time, these open and frank discussions are held in my presence, where I can referee, cajole, support and sometimes even confront my clients who stall or their family members who stonewall. I generally take this approach rather than coaching in one of two instances. One is when I have concluded that either the family would be too formidable for my client to take on alone or when I'm not certain that my client would risk being vulnerable with emotions, rather than merely conducting a safe but unproductive intellectualized discussion. Adequate preparation for these sessions is essential to their success. With some clients, this can take months; with others, it can take only weeks. I basically ask clients to clarify in advance their answer to three questions: What do you need to say to your parents or other family members? What do you need to hear from them? Where do you want to start? For a more detailed discussion of this technique, readers may wish to refer to the chapter on this technique in my previous book.[9]

A note of caution: Therapists wishing to implement this technique need to assess carefully and make a clinical judgment about whether they feel their client will be re-injured by an oblivious or self-interested parent, seek vengeance on their parents, or need the support and even advocacy of having this talk in your presence. Those who seem up to the task of having such a conversation alone are urged to do so. Furthermore, sometimes having a supportive spouse accompany a client suffices, as it did for Melanie and Anthony in chapter 2, once I had coached them. The primary advantage to this strategy is that people who need a boost have the advantage of having such a conversation under your watchful eye.

What Is the Role of Countertransference?

In the psychoanalytic literature, transference is defined as the unresolved feelings that clients unconsciously transfer onto the therapist from another significant person in their life. In this way, the therapist becomes a surrogate or stand-in for these other significant people, as the client begins to play out old dynamics. In contrast, countertransference is defined as the therapist's own personal experiences that become activated in response to the patient.[10] In either case, these reactions likely are anachronistic and at least need to be examined, if not changed. For our purposes, I will confine this discussion to countertransference.

Countertransference is not always bad. Absolutely not. In fact, part of the reason that my sleuthing paid off so well and so quickly with Karla and Marty was my own countertransference. I had been where they were, so I readily recognized their issues. Countertransference, *when it is appropriately understood and managed*, gives the therapist a third eye and ear that assist in discerning what clients really are saying. A therapist's personal knowledge also can be extremely helpful in identifying when grief is embedded in clients' symptoms since for most, it is so deeply embedded that they have no conscious access to the loss or to its impact. Further, when therapists share their own experience using appropriate self-disclosure, what enables them to do this with a therapeutic outcome is thorough knowledge of and effective management of their countertransferences. Of course, a therapist's own issues can become a blind spot, causing him or her to identify an issue that does not exist or overlook one that does. This is why it is important that, even though I believe that loss is a master issue that underlies a variety of seemingly unrelated clinical presentations, it is important to underscore that I am willing to abandon that premise when I find no evidence to substantiate it.

The effective, ethical use of countertransference requires a high degree of self-knowledge on the part of the therapist. And sadly, like my colleague in training who contended that he finished grieving for his father in an afternoon, too many clinicians have a limited degree of self-awareness of their own father loss, a situation which I hope this book will help remedy. Nor have they developed a process of identifying and managing these interfaces of clients' issues with their own when they occur. This, then, renders them ineffective at best or harmful at worst. Therapists who have not themselves adequately grieved either will get caught up in their own emotional reverberations as clients begin to grieve, or they will subtly cue clients to keep their feelings and their experience to themselves. Either way, these therapists render themselves ineffective. A further problem with unaddressed and poorly understood countertransference reactions is the tendency, when treating people with issues or pathology similar to your own family, is for you to be vulnerable to being inducted into their dysfunctional system. This, too, ties your hands.

Because father loss is such an emotionally charged issue, which makes it is especially important to identify potential countertransferences, I would offer readers some questions to ponder:

1. How did the people in your family of origin handle strong emotions such as anger or sadness?
2. What messages did the people in your family give you regarding how loss was to be handled?
3. What messages did you get regarding asking for help?
4. What were you told or shown about needing or being needy?
5. In your family, did you get any different messages about physical distress compared with emotional distress?

The overall purpose in these musings is for you to begin to identify their template for what is acceptable and unacceptable behavior. Without this knowledge, it will be difficult to make certain your preferences for what is appropriate or your therapeutic style are not imposed on clients. As Jeannette Kramer indicated in her authoritative text on therapist-client interfaces that result in therapists' countertransferences:

> When a therapist meets a family, he brings his unique learnings from his own background, as the family brings theirs. The therapist is also a member of a family with a tendency to repeat the same patterns in different systems, just as clients do. He carries his own bias, like a filter, so that he is susceptible to setting up the reality he treats.[11]

Conclusion

For most who have experienced a loss, coming to accept their situation is a key outcome of a healthy grief process. Then, people no longer are plagued by internal sentences that previously haunted them, like "Why?" or "Why me?" or "If only . . ." Usually, applying any or all of the techniques just discussed eventually allows people to put their pain to rest. But the only recourse of some others is to accept the unfairness and the uncertainties inherent in their situation. In those instances, the Serenity Prayer, a kind of mantra for Alcoholics Anonymous can be helpful. I have plaques of this slogan in both of my offices. Sometimes, this and instilling the hope that it will be different once clients have accepted the unacceptable are all that we can offer. But those are not trivial offerings.

Father loss and the spiritual crisis that so often accompanies it are a crucible. Resolving father loss clearly is painful for clients; sharing in their process often is poignant for therapists. Each time I am invited into people's process to identify the source of their pain and to share in its resolution, I know I have entered sacred ground. Taking their journey with them is a privilege; seeing the rebirth that is possible as a result is exhilarating. It is a clinical experience that is second to none.

References

1. Robert Goulding and Mary Goulding, *Changing Lives Through Redecision Therapy* (New York: Bruner/Mazel, 1979), 6.

2. Janet Johnston and Linda Campbell, *Impasses of Divorce* (New York: Free Press, 1988), 61.

3. Norman Paul and Betty Paul, *The Marital Puzzle: Transgenerational Analysis of Marriage Counseling* (New York: Gardner, 1986), 16.

4. Beth Erickson, "An Evaluation of a Curriculum Intervention: Conceptual Development in In-Service Educators" (Ph.D. diss., University of Minnesota, 1976).

5. Herb Goldberg, *The Inner Male: Overcoming Roadblocks to Intimacy* (New York: Signet, 1987), 85.

6. Evan Imber-Black and Janine Roberts, *Rituals in Our Times: Celebrating, Healing and Changing Our Lives and Relationships* (New York: Harper Perennial, 1992).

7. Murray Bowen, *Family Therapy in Clinical Practice* (New York: Jason Aronson, 1978), 1.

8. James Framo, "You Can and Should Go Home Again," in *Explorations in Marital and Family Therapy* (New York: Springer, 1982), 175–216; and *Family-of-Origin Therapy* (New York: Bruner/Mazel, 1992), 2.

9. Beth Erickson, "The Major Surgery of Psychotherapy: The Extended Family of Origin Session," in *Helping Men Change: The Role of the Female Therapist* (Newbury Park, Calif.: Sage Publications, 1993), 397–420.

10. Ibid., 51.

11. Jeannette Kramer, *Family Interfaces: Transgenerational Patterns* (New York: Bruner/Mazel, 1985), 44.

Appendix C:
To Therapists on the Spiritual Crises in Father Loss

The following are some special considerations that apply to therapists and counselors from all disciplines; these are effective with clients who need our help to grapple with the spiritual dilemmas inherent in father loss.

1. It is important to do our own grief work. Otherwise, it will be extremely difficult to help—or even to allow—clients to do their own. If we deny our own need to come to grips with our own relationship with our father, whether consciously or unconsciously, we will likely have a blind spot related to these issues. Naturally, we will wish to continue to keep them out of sight and out of mind so our own scars do not begin to ache. So we silently will cue clients that their loss is

not appropriate or necessary material to discuss. Yet, when an unresolved loss fuels people's dysfunction, unless that loss is addressed and resolved, clients' pain will persist. Perhaps this is a major contributor to the revolving door of mental health services that so many benefactors decry.

2. While shepherding clients through this spiritual passage may seem difficult if you are unclear about your own faith, it may be even more difficult if you are. It is too tempting to use this opportunity to be an evangelist who converts vulnerable clients. For those whose practice of religion presses for conversion to "the one true faith," it may be difficult indeed to resist the temptation to attempt to win another convert. It may be easier to wade into deep waters with clients if we know multiple strokes to swim.

3. The quest for spiritual communion and clarity is so fundamental to the human experience that it can be and is experienced by Christians, Jews, Moslems, Buddhists, Shintoists and even atheists. It is important to be careful not to make this struggle into one of dogma or doctrine. It is not. Rather, it is about basic human dilemmas and existential issues.

4. Feel free to make specific references related to people's particular religious bent or affiliation, once you determine that they have one. Doing so can help them grasp these very abstract, ephemeral ideas. For example, with Jews, I talk of the Prayer for the Dead, or Kaddish, of sitting shivah to mark the loss, and of Yom Kippur, the Day of Atonement. For Christians when discussing

forgiveness, I might refer to confession, redemption or the rebirth and resurrection that are inherent in fresh starts. With Buddhists, I might suggest that they seek answers to their questions about meaning through mindfulness and meditation. It is important to note that these references are used to bring elements of their faith or tradition into the therapeutic process that might facilitate their spiritual quest, not for the therapist to gain a convert.

5. Do not underestimate the power of simply being with clients in the angst of their grief and their existential journey. If one of the reasons that a loss is not resolved at the time it occurs is clients being left alone with it, then our willingness to go with clients in their journey, as far as the path permits, can be healing itself. We cannot resolve a loss for clients. And we can only offer our willingness to empathize and be with them, because it is not our struggle. But this with-ness is a powerful tonic for most as we bear witness to their pain.

6. Expect to feel overwhelmed. In the face of tragedy, everyone experiences not knowing what to say. So sometimes saying "Ouch!" or "I'm so sorry!" can be profound. I am not afraid to dab genuine tears that come as I listen to a client's pain. This demonstration of empathy is more powerful than hundreds of words ever will be. It can be therapeutic when we admit feeling overwhelmed, even though it is not our story. This can help clients feel more normal at a time when nothing feels normal. Perhaps what will help therapists most is to remember that they cannot fix this conundrum because it is not theirs to fix.

7. If a client's situation stirs up more for you than a few tears, it probably has hooked vestiges of your own issues with your father. Rather than feeling guilty or ashamed of that, use it as an opportunity to finish another piece. Doing so is important for your own health as well as for your therapeutic effectiveness. So take some time after the session to find out what those feelings have tapped for you. Sit and reflect. Write about it. Cry. And don't be afraid to seek the consultation of a trusted colleague if these feelings linger for more than a few minutes after they are piqued.

8. If you end up carrying clients' hurt home with you, be careful of compassion fatigue. Those of us who must endure and report on others' trauma on a daily basis are highly susceptible to burning out from it. So learn strategies for taking care of yourself and do so on a regular basis, particularly after difficult sessions.

The questions people ask themselves are very personal, individual questions for which there are no pat answers. And it is folly to pretend that there are or that one has them. Therapists who are granted the privilege of sharing clients' struggles must be mindful that all roads lead to Rome and avoid foisting on clients a pat road map.

Appendix D:
Twelve Ts for Structuring Treatment to Resolve Father Loss

1. **Treat** the cause, rather than merely the symptoms.

2. **Timing** is everything, so hurry slowly.

3. In the beginning, lay **tracks to** and do **touch-and-go landings** about the loss.

4. Help clients **take responsibility** for their feelings, rather than blame.

5. Understanding and managing **transference and countertransference** are essential.

6. Effective resolution of father loss equals **tears** plus fresh insight.

7. Help patients create new **thought patterns** about the loss.

8. Guide patients to **talk with,** not confront, their parents.

9. When the necessary groundwork has been laid, help the patient rework the **trauma** at its source.

10. **Trance work** such as hypnosis, paradox, open-chair dialogues, and visualizations help patients rework trauma and create new endings.

11. Help patients find **transcendent meaning** for the trauma.

12. Effective treatment of so painful an issue requires **teamwork** and collaboration between therapist and client.

Remember, it's never too late to have a good childhood.

Suggested Reading

Ackerman, Nathan. *The Psychodynamics of Family Life.* New York: Basic Books, 1958.

Ackerman, Robert. *Perfect Daughters: Adult Children of Alcoholics.* Deerfield Beach, Fla.: Health Communications, 1989.

Berkus, Rusty. *To Heal Again: Towards Serenity and the Resolution of Grief.* Encino, Calif.: Red Rose Press, 1984.

Blankenhorn, David. *Fatherless America: Confronting Our Most Urgent Social Problem.* New York: Basic Books, 1995.

Bly, Robert. *A Gathering of Men: With Bill Moyers and Robert Bly.* New York: Mystic Fire Video, 1989.

Bowen, Murray. *Family Therapy in Clinical Practice.* New York: Jason Aronson, 1978.

Carter, Elizabeth, and Monica McGoldrick, *The Family Life Cycle: A Framework for Family Therapy.* New York: Gardner, 1980.

Erickson, Beth. *Helping Men Change: The Role of the Female Therapist.* Newbury Park, Calif.: Sage Publications, 1993.

Framo, James. *Explorations in Marital and Family Therapy.* New York: Springer, 1982.

_____. *Family-of-Origin Therapy.* New York: Bruner/Mazel, 1992.

Frankl, Viktor. *Man's Search for Meaning: An Introduction to Logotherapy.* New York: Washington Square Press, 1959.

Galston, William. "Divorce American Style." *Public Interest* 126 (Summer 1996): 12–26.

Goldberg, Herb. *The Inner Male: Overcoming Roadblocks to Intimacy.* New York: Signet, 1987.

Golomb, Elana. *Trapped in the Mirror: Adult Children of Narcissists in Their Struggle for Self.* New York: William Morrow, 1992.

Goulding, Robert, and Mary Goulding. *Changing Lives Through Redecision Therapy.* New York: Bruner/Mazel, 1979.

Imber-Black, Evan, and Janine Roberts. *Rituals in Our Times: Celebrating, Healing and Changing Our Lives and Relationships.* New York: Harper Perennial, 1992.

Johnston, Janet, and Linda Campbell. *Impasses of Divorce.* New York: Free Press, 1988.

Keen, Sam. *Fire in the Belly: On Being a Man.* New York: Bantam, 1991.

Kramer, Jeannette. *Family Interfaces: Transgenerational Patterns.* New York: Bruner/Mazel, 1985.

Kushner, Harold. *When Bad Things Happen to Good People.* New York: Schocken, 1981.

Lewis, C. S. *A Grief Observed.* New York: Bantam Books, 1961.

Lifton, Betty Jean. *Lost and Found: The Adoption Experience.* New York: Harper & Row, 1988.

Mahler, Margaret, Fred Pine, and Anni Bergman. *The Psychological Birth of the Human Infant.* New York: Basic Books, 1975.

Maine, Margo. *Father Hunger: Fathers, Daughters and Food.* Carlsbad, Calif.: Gurze Books, 1991.

Moore, Robert, and Douglas Gillette. *King, Warrior, Magician, Lover: Rediscovering the Archetypes of the Mature Masculine.* San Francisco: Harper San Francisco, 1990.

Myss, Caroline. *Anatomy of the Spirit: The Seven Stages of Power and Healing.* Boulder, Colorado: Sounds True Audio, 1996.

Osherson, Samuel. *Finding Our Fathers: The Unfinished Business of Manhood.* New York: Free Press, 1986.

_____. *Wrestling with Love: How Men Struggle with Intimacy.* New York: Fawcett Columbine, 1992.

Paul, Norman, and Betty Paul. *The Marital Puzzle: Transgenerational Analysis of Marriage Counseling.* New York: Gardner, 1986.

Pipher, Mary. *Reviving Ophelia.* San Francisco: Harper San Francisco, 1996.

Pipher, Mary. *The Shelter of Each Other: Rebuilding Our Families.* New York: G. P. Putnam's Sons, 1996.

Piaget, Jean. *The Moral Judgment of the Child.* 1932. Reprint, Glencoe, Ill.: Free Press, 1948.

Pittman, Frank. *Man Enough: Fathers, Sons and the Search for Masculinity.* New York: G. P. Putman's Sons, 1993.

Popenoe, David. *Life Without Father.* New York: Free Press, 1996

Progoff, Ira. *At a Journal Workshop: The Basic Text and Guide for Using the Intensive Journal.* New York: Dialogue House Library, 1975.

Redfield, James. *The Celestine Prophecy.* New York: Bantam Books, 1994.

Strong, Bryan, and Christine DeVault. *The Marriage and Family Experience,* 5th ed. St. Paul: West Publishing, 1992.

Truax, C. B., and Robert Carkoff. *Effective Counseling and Psychotherapy.* Chicago: Aldine, 1967.

Viorst, Judith. *Necessary Losses.* New York: Fawcett Gold Medal, 1986.

Viscott, David. *Emotional Resilience: Simple Truths for Dealing with the Unfinished Business of Your Past.* New York: Random House Audiobooks, 1996.

Wallerstein, Judith, and Sandra Blakeslee. *Second Chances: Men, Women and Children a Decade After Divorce.* New York: Ticknor & Fields, 1989.

Walsch, Neale Donald. *Conversations with God, I and II.* Charlotteville, Va.: Hampton Roads Publishing, 1996.

Whitehead, Barbara. "Dan Quayle Was Right." *Atlantic Monthly,* April 1993.

Wiesel, Elie. *Night.* New York: Bantam Books, 1960.

Index

Author's Note

I sincerely hope this book has been meaningful to you. I would be delighted to hear how you use this book or if there is a way I might further help you on your journey.

I am available for lectures, seminars, training, supervision, consultation, personal coaching and psychotherapy. Those wanting to share or wishing for information about my services may contact me at:

Beth M. Erickson, Ph.D.
1875 Forest Circle
Santa Fe, New Mexico 87505
Phone: (800) 292-0500 or (505) 983-0500
Fax: (505) 983-0400
E-mail: drbeth@drbeth.com
Web site: www.drbeth.com